OSPREY
MILITARY

CAMPAIGN SERIES 22

QADESH 1300BC

D0619682

GENERAL EDITOR DAVID G. CHANDLER

OSPREY MILITARY

CAMPAIGN SERIES 22

QADESH 1300BC

CLASH OF THE WARRIOR KINGS

MARK HEALY

◀ *It was in the fifth year of his reign that the Pharaoh Rameses II engaged the army of the Hittite king Muwatallish at Qadesh on the Orontes in one of the great battles of antiquity. Characterized by the clash of masses of chariots, it was also the high-water mark of the form of warfare practised during the Late Bronze Age in the Ancient Near East. The Egyptians and Hittites were the foremost exponents of chariot warfare at this time, and Qadesh was notable for the manner in which both sides sought to impose their will upon the other by the employment of distinctive chariot tactics that had evolved over some centuries. This could not be better shown than in this relief from the Pharaoh's funerary temple, known as the Rameseum*

at Thebes. On the left of the register can be seen the lighter, two-man Egyptian chariots with the heavier, three-man chariots of the Hittites shown on the right. Once Pharaoh's forces had rallied, following the surprise Hittite attack, and contained the weight and power of the close-combat tactics of their chariotry, the crews of the rapid-manoeuvring Egyptian machines were able to employ their powerful composite bows to execute fearful destruction among the slower-moving Hittite ranks. In this way what appeared initially as a remarkable Hittite strategic triumph at Qadesh may have been transformed, on the battlefield, into a tactical Egyptian victory.

▲ *Tell Nebi-Mend, the ancient Qadesh (Hittite Kinza) on the Orontes. Dominating the skyline, it is seen here from the eastern side and gives a view of the site as seen from the Hittite perspective. Beyond lies the plain on which the battle was fought. Its extent and eminent suitability for the employment of massed chariots can be clearly seen and goes some way to supporting the view that Qadesh was a designated arena for the* great contest of arms between the Nilotic empire and that of Hatti. Rameses' camp would have lain out of sight beyond the tell. The Hittite chariot assault, whatever its strength, would have been launched to the south of the tell which is on the left of the picture. (P.Parr)

First published in 1993 by Osprey Publishing Ltd, 59 Grosvenor Street, London W1X 9DA.

ISBN 1-85532-300-1
Produced by DAG Publications Ltd for Osprey Publishing Ltd.
Colour bird's eye view illustrations by Peter Harper.
Wargaming Qadesh by Ken Antcliff
Wargames consultant Duncan Macfarlane.
Cartography by Micromap.
Mono camerawork by M&E Reproductions, North Fambridge, Essex.
Printed and bound in Hong Kong.

CONTENTS

Acknowledgements
The framework for this text draws heavily on the interpretation of Qadesh suggested by the Egyptologist Hans Goedicke. His is the only account of the 'battle' that I find remotely credible; responsibility for the flesh on the skeleton, however, is mine as are any errors. I wish to thank Christine el Mahdy for her encouragement, help and freely given time spent listening to the meanderings of a non Egyptologist, and Mr Peter Parr of the Institute of Archaeology, University College London, who so very kindly proffered valuable information concerning the battle site, and allowed me to use photographs taken during his many years of excavations at Qadesh.

INTRODUCTION

It is a measure of the fascination exerted by the Battle of Qadesh that nearly three and a quarter millennia after the event it still excites the interest of scholar and layman alike. That this should be so is not surprising. This clash of arms was the penultimate act of a drama whose initial scenes were played out during the great power conflicts and rivalries that characterized the contest for the mastery of Syria in the Ancient Near East during the 14th and 13th centuries BC. It is the stuff of the waxing and waning of empires, and of kings who bestrode their time as colossi, ultimate practitioners of a form of warfare soon to be eclipsed with the onset of the age of iron.

Qadesh is the earliest battle in the history of mankind whose course can be reliably reconstructed in detail. It has in consequence been frequently described in many works on warfare and ancient history. A notable feature of these many narratives is that they offer a fairly uniform picture of the battle. These accounts nearly all share a generally uncritical, almost literal reading and acceptance of the veracity of the Rameside sources and their translations wherein concerns for philological exactitude

▶ *During the second half of the second millennium the Ancient Near East witnessed a prolonged and sometimes bitter contest between the great powers of the day as they vied for control of Syria. During that period the kingdom of Egypt had retained a consistent interest in the region, contending first with the Kingdom of Mitanni and, from the mid 14th century onwards, its Anatolian successor, the Hittite empire. Although driven by more particular national interests, all three kingdoms shared a common desire to control the region in order to exploit its great material wealth and the immensely profitable international trade that turned Syria into the crossroads of the Ancient World. The Nilotic kingdom had always had a major interest in the region and evidence of trade with Byblos extends as far back as the 1st Dynasty. However, the defining feature of Egypt's interest in the Levant during the New Kingdom period (c.1565-1085) arose in the wake of the expulsion of the Hyksos invaders in the 16th century The development of a defensive military strategy that saw the projection and maintenance of Egyptian military power as far north as Syria was perceived as the best means of ensuring the security of her eastern borders. Although military power was the basis of Egypt's imperialism in Canaan and the Levant, throughout the New Kingdom it was always a minimalist policy. The prime concern was to ensure the regular payment of tribute from the vassal states within the empire and as long as this continued the Nilotic rulers maintained a loose rein over their Asiatic provinces. The petty states within the 'empire' were free to conduct their own*

internecine wars. But their allegiances were fickle. When strong military demonstrations were not forthcoming to remind them of where their loyalties lay, they schemed with Egypt's enemies to overthrow the yoke of pharaoh. First Mitanni and later Hatti sought to undermine Egyptian power in central Syria. Where ill-defined or contested boundaries between the spheres of interest of these powers in this vital region led to instability, therein lay the opportunity for vassal kingdoms to stir up trouble by playing off one power against the other. The prolonged military campaigning of Tuthmosis III in northern Syria was designed to ensure permanent Egyptian control of the region, but this could not be maintained because Syria was more than 600 miles from the Nilotic kingdom. The permanent and substantial military presence required to preserve a firm Egyptian grip on the region was not a price she was prepared or able to pay. Resolution of the long-drawn-out conflict with Mitanni by treaty in the reign of Tuthmosis IV defined the borders between the two empires and provided three generations of peace. With the overthrow of Mitanni by the Hittites in the mid 14th century the problem once more revived. The reticence of the later pharaohs of the 18th Dynasty to use military power in Syria saw Egyptian influence and territory slip away in the face of Hittite gains. But with the accession of the 19th Dynasty there was begun a new policy, predicated on revived military power that sought to strengthen Egypt's control over her Asiatic possessions and eventually recover the 'lost' lands of central Syria.

have taken precedence over reconstructions of the battle that take seriously the contingencies of warfare in the Late Bronze Age. As this 'Campaign' title will argue for a different understanding of what occurred at Qadesh by considering seriously such matters, it is necessary by way of an introduction to offer a résumé of the traditional accounts of the battle. This will allow the reader to gain an appreciation of how the critical analysis and account contained herein leads to a markedly different interpretation of the events that occurred in Syria more than

three thousand years ago.

In essence an iteration of the accounts that are presented in most texts tell the following story: The army of Rameses II advanced upon the city of Qadesh in four corps. Pharaoh was with the corps of Amun, which was in the van of the Egyptian army. While crossing the River Orontes to begin the approach to the city from the south, two bedouin tribesmen in the employ of Hatti led the gullible Rameses to believe that the Hittite army was many miles away to the north. Rameses, believing he had

The Contest for Syria

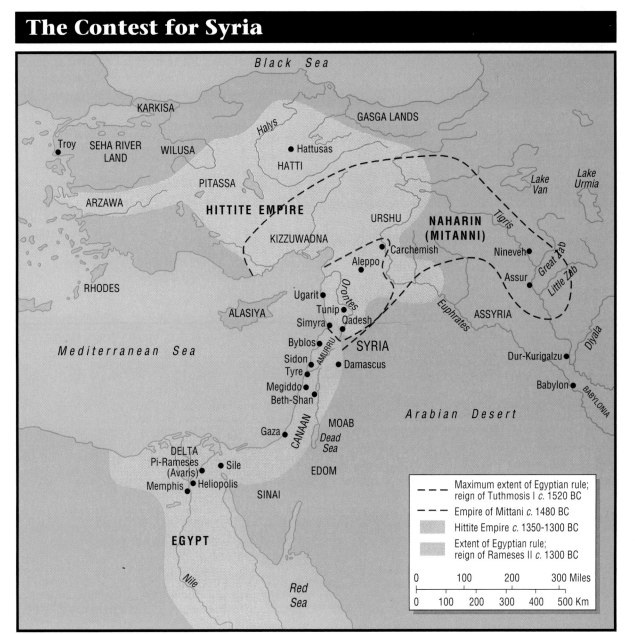

stolen a march on the Hittite king Muwatallish and therefore secured the strategic advantage over his enemy, ordered Amun forward and on to the city without further ado. Having established camp to the north-west of Qadesh, Pharaoh was then mightily unnerved to discover that not only had the Hittite army already arrived, but was even then drawn up for battle and hidden behind the great mound on which Qadesh was built.

Having dispatched his Vizier to hurry on the second corps of P'Re (The Re), it was then ambushed

▲ *Regarded by many as the greatest of all the pharaohs of Egypt, Tuthmosis III (1504-1450) carved out the Egyptian Empire in Canaan and the Levant. Under his aegis the Egyptian army became the greatest war* *machine of its time and the Nilotic kingdom the foremost power of the age. His achievements spurred the martial ambitions of the young Rameses II who desired to emulate those of his great 18th-Dynasty forebear.*

as it marched across the Plain of Qadesh. The entire corps disintegrated in panic as a force of 2,500 Hittite chariots, which had been lying in wait, crossed a ford of the Orontes and hurled itself at the Egyptian column. The Hittite host then turned north and attacked Amun's camp. Many of the Hittites, having broken through the shield wall, succumbed to the lure of the booty of the camp. As with P'Re, many of Amun's troops panicked and abandoned Rameses to his fate. Pharaoh, however, donning his armour, leapt into his chariot and then almost single-handedly held off the Hittite chariotry, inflicting heavy losses on them. The Hittite monarch, overlooking the battlefield and surrounded by his uncommitted infantry, ordered a further 1,000 chariots to the aid of the first wave who now, because of the valour of Rameses, were in a dire predicament. Just as the Hittite reinforcement reached the camp, Pharaoh was saved by the arrival of the Ne'arin. These were a body of troops that, earlier on, unbeknown to the Hittites, Pharaoh had detached from the main body of the Egyptian army and ordered to approach Qadesh from the north. With their arrival Rameses was able to see off the Hittite attack. Many high-ranking Hittite and allied warriors lay dead on the plain and many more were chased into Qadesh or suffered the humiliation of having to swim across the Orontes to escape the wrath of Rameses. Some accounts see the combat as having continued into the second day, but as a consequence of the bravery of Pharaoh and the dire losses among the Hittite chariotry, Muwatallish offered Rameses a truce on the following day. This accepted, the two armies withdrew to their homelands.

Such are the essential elements of the Battle of Qadesh as commonly presented. While this account will accept much of the above as a framework, there are more than a few anomalies in the Rameside sources to be addressed. When these are explored from a military rather than linguistic perspective they offer the possibility of a different account of the Battle of Qadesh. Such an account requires an appreciation of the antecedents of this battle, however, and these are to be found on the wider stage of the complex international politics of the great powers of the day and the relations with their lesser but duplicitous vassal kingdoms in the Ancient Near East.

Syria: Arena of the Ancient Near East

The prolonged interest of the great powers of the Ancient Near East in Syria derived from their respective desires to dominate and exploit the economic resources and trade of the region. During this period Syria was the crossroads of world commerce. Goods from the Aegean and beyond entered the Near East via ports such as Ugarit, whose ships dominated maritime trade in the eastern Mediterranean. Underwater excavations of Late Bronze Age ships such as that discovered near Cape Gelidonya off the south coast of Turkey, show the remarkable range of goods they carried — copper, tin, chemicals, tools, glass ingots, ivory, faience, jewellery, luxury goods, timber, textiles and foodstuffs. This merchandise was then distributed throughout the Near East and beyond by a network of extensive trade routes. From the east and south, these same land routes were used by merchants who brought raw materials such as precious metals, tin, copper, lapis lazuli and other merchandise from as far afield as Iran and Afghanistan to trade in the emporia of Syria. With its inherent fertility and richness in natural resources, Syria therefore offered much to predatory powers seeking to use such wealth for their own benefit. Thirty-three centuries ago 'world' power was synonymous with the control of Syria, so it is not surprising that for nearly two hundred years the 'great powers' of Egypt, Mitanni and Hatti expended much blood and treasure in wars designed to ensure their respective control of this vitally strategic region. While this provides the backdrop to general great power motivation in Syria, it is possible, within this wider context, to identify a more specific sequence of events that was to culminate in the Battle of Qadesh.

In the first half of the 14th century the Hittite kingdom under its vigorous monarch Suppiluliumas began a systematic and highly successful demolition of the position of the Kingdom of Mitanni in northern Syria. The immediate fallout was the unravelling of the international status quo that had obtained in the region since the peace treaty between Egypt and the Kingdom of Mitanni concluded during the reign of Tuthmosis IV (1425-17) some two generations before. Indeed, it had been an earlier if fitful revival of the power of the Anatolian kingdom that

had prompted the *rapprochement* between the two rival powers after many decades of warfare in Syria. It was a treaty that served the interests of both powers at the time. For Egypt, notwithstanding the prodigious military efforts of Tuthmosis III and his son Amenophis II, had witnessed a progressive loss of ground to Mitanni in the region. Mitanni, in the wake of the revival of her near and powerful Anatolian neighbour, faced the very real prospect of a two-front war. Pondering the alternatives, Saussatar, King of Mitanni, determined to eliminate his southern front by approaching the Nilotic kingdom with a formal offer of 'brotherhood' that would secure a cessation of hostilities in Syria and conclude an alliance between Mitanni and Egypt. There was every reason to believe that such a treaty would be perceived as being in Egypt's interest. Sometime after year ten of Amenophis II's reign, '... the Chiefs of Mitanni came to him, their tribute upon their backs, to seek the peace of his majesty'.

The treaty was finally concluded in the reigns of the respective successors of the two kings, when Tuthmosis IV married the daughter of Artatama of Mitanni. The most significant matter agreed by both parties was the clear demarcation of the borders between the two empires in central Syria. While no copy of the treaty itself has yet been recovered, the specific details of the boundaries can be inferred from later documents (see map on page 10). It did, however, recognize Egypt's claim to Amurru, the strategically vital Eleutheros valley and Qadesh. The formalization of these borders entailed the Egyptians surrendering claims to territories that had once fallen within their imperial domain by virtue of the conquests of Tuthmosis I and III. In essence the boundaries finally a.greed corresponded to those of Egypt and Mitanni extant on the death of Amenophis II. Their real significance for the Nilotic kingdom lay in the manner whereby during the next two hundred years, down to the time of Rameses II, they became impressed on the Egyptian mind as permanent and fixed. Indeed, the perception that these borders marked the true boundaries of the Nilotic empire meant that Egypt would in all likelihood take strong measures against any power encroaching upon them.

In the decades that followed, Mitanni and Egypt reaped the dividends of this prolonged peace. Dur-

The Post-Treaty Border of Egypt and Mitanni in Syria, *c.* 1417 BC

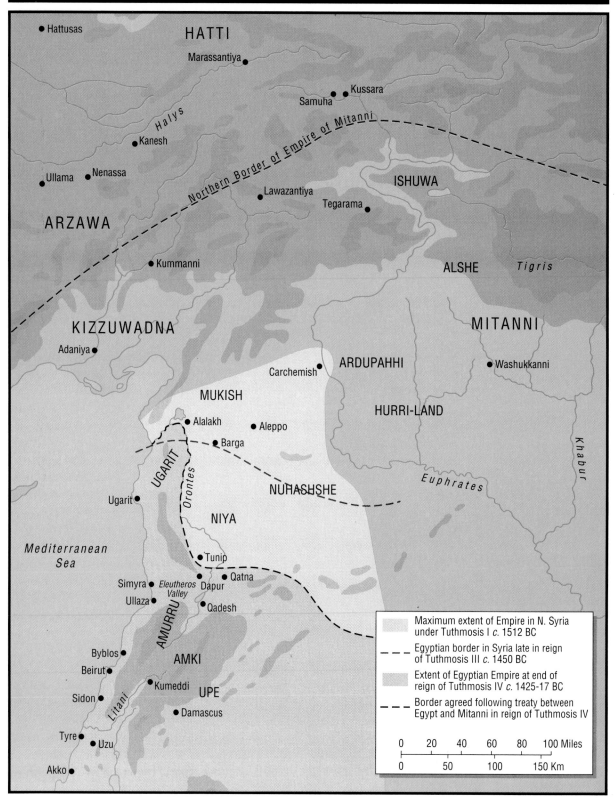

Hattusas

HATTI

Marassantiya

Kussara
Samuha

Halys

Kanesh

Ullama Nenassa

ARZAWA

Lawazantiya

ISHUWA

Tegarama

Kummanni

ALSHE *Tigris*

KIZZUWADNA

MITANNI

Adaniya

Carchemish ARDUPAHHI

Washukkanni

MUKISH

HURRI-LAND

Alalakh Aleppo

Barga

UGARIT

Orontes

NUHASHSHE

Euphrates

Khabur

Ugarit

NIYA

*Mediterranean
Sea*

Tunip

Simyra *Eleutheros
Valley* Dapur Qatna

Ullaza

AMURRU Qadesh

Byblos

AMKI

Beirut

Kumeddi UPE

Sidon

Litani

Damascus

Tyre
Uzu

Akko

Maximum extent of Empire in N. Syria under Tuthmosis I *c.* 1512 BC	
— — — Egyptian border in Syria late in reign of Tuthmosis III *c.* 1450 BC	
Extent of Egyptian Empire at end of reign of Tuthmosis IV *c.* 1425-17 BC	
– – – Border agreed following treaty between Egypt and Mitanni in reign of Tuthmosis IV	

0	20	40	60	80	100 Miles
0		50	100		150 Km

ing this period the wealth and prosperity of New Kingdom Egypt reached its apogee. Tribute poured in from her Canaanite possessions and the secure borders with Mitanni allowed for the unimpeded movement of goods along the trade routes. For three decades this relative tranquillity lasted, with the whole of the Fertile Crescent seemingly at peace as a consequence of the great power axis of Egypt, Mitanni and Kassite Babylon.

Amurru: The Strategic Marchland

To access their central Syrian dependencies on the Orontes from the ports on the coast the Egyptians depended upon the land corridor provided by the Eleutheros valley which ran through the territory known colloquially as 'Amurru'. In times past Egyptian armies had marched through the Eleutheros valley before embarking upon their assault on Mitanni's possessions in northern Syria. While the strategic importance of this route could not be denied, its retention in Egyptian hands hinged in turn on the Nilotic kingdom's possession of the city of Qadesh on the Orontes. Qadesh was so placed that not only did it dominate the western end of the Eleutheros valley, but it also lay astride the main Egyptian invasion route to the north Syrian plain. Any attempt to bring northern Syria within the borders of the Nilotic empire presupposed Egyptian possession of Qadesh. Following the peace treaty

◀ The most important aspect of the treaty that concluded the 'brotherhood' between Egypt and Mitanni was the clear demarcation of their respective imperial borders in Syria. Although acceptance of this line required Egypt to forego her claim to cities and territories (see area on map) that had fallen within the domain of her rule during the reign of Tuthmosis III and Amenophis II, she had in reality been losing ground to Mitanni in these regions for some time.

This clear demarcation allowed Egypt to eschew the need for military demonstrations to convince her Syrian vassals of continued loyalty as both powers agreed not to undermine their respective spheres of influence. As a consequence no Egyptian army campaigned in Syria for some sixty years following the treaty's conclusion. This stability was only undermined when the Hittites proceeded to destroy the position of Mitanni in northern Syria.

with Mitanni, Egypt's perception of these possessions in such terms faded as her rulers reconciled themselves to the loss of the former north Syrian territories. However, it followed that if at any time in the future Egypt should revive her imperial aspirations in that region, their strategic significance would once again come to the fore. It was the importance of Qadesh and Amurru and their respective ownership that was to become the spur to the ultimate conflict between Egypt and Hatti.

It was the precision with which the territories of Mitanni and Egypt were formally demarcated by treaty that accounted for the longevity of the peace between the two powers. The settlement of vassal ownership of the border kingdoms removed the potential sources of conflict between the two empires. But the emergence of a nascent political entity calling itself 'Amurru' during the reign of Amenophis III caused no little difficulty for both Egypt and Mitanni. Although regarded as a nominal Egyptian possession, Amurru was not perceived by either empire as a legitimate kingdom for it had not existed at the time the peace treaty was concluded. Nevertheless, under the strong leadership of the dynamic figure of one Abdi-Ashirta and later his son Aziru, the disparate inhabitants of the region acquired a measure of political coherence that had enabled them, by the end of the 14th century, to create a kingdom that occupied all the lands between the Mediterranean Sea and the Orontes valley. There can be no doubting that Abdi-Ashirta and his son were both wily, politically ingenious, but self-serving individuals. While outwardly professing loyalty to his overlord Amenophis III in Egypt, Abdi-Ashirta nevertheless took advantage of the Nilotic kingdom's relative indifference to its imperial possessions to expand his kingdom. The lack of an effective Egyptian military presence in the region allowed Abdi-Ashirta to impose his will on surrounding territories, some of whom appealed in vain to Egypt to help them fight this local strongman.

It is a measure of the difficulty Amurru caused the great powers that Mitanni deemed it necessary to take military action to control this nominally Egyptian 'vassal'. Egypt did eventually bestir itself and sent a military expedition, and the problem of Amurru was temporarily removed by the death of Abdi-Ashirta, but matters on the wider stage now

◄ *While it is now clear that the Egyptian empire in the Levant did not crumble during the reign of Amenophis IV, better known as Akhenaten (1353-35), important territories were lost to the revivified Hittite empire under its dynamic king Suppiluliumas. These were the city of Qadesh on the Orontes, an Egyptian possession since the days of Amenophis II, and the strategically important marchland of Amurru.*

proceeded to bring to an end the generations-long accord between Egypt and Mitanni and in the process create the conditions for the revival of Amurru.

Suppiluliumas the Great

It is not the place here to examine in detail the Hittite takeover of northern Syria, but rather to see how the consequences arising therefrom affected the relations between Egypt and Hatti and how in turn these would culminate in the Battle of Qadesh.

The accession of Suppiluliumas can only be dated to approximately 1380. That he came to the throne determined to assert the Hittite claim to Syria seems certain, as hostilities with Mitanni broke out shortly thereafter. In his first Syrian campaign he conquered the states of Aleppo, Alalakh, Nuhashshe and Tunip in northern Syria. An attempt by Mitanni in the following decade to reassert her power among her former vassals, now linked by treaty to Hatti, was utilized by the Hittite monarch as a *casus belli* and the second Syrian war was launched. Declaring the former Mitannian vassal kingdoms to be rebels, Suppiluliumas crossed the River

Euphrates into the land of Ishuwa, marched directly south and, having totally surprised Mitanni, attacked it directly and in a very rapid campaign occupied and sacked the capital Washukkanni. Turning west, the Hittite monarch recrossed the Euphrates and entered Syria, his true objective, to the south of Carchemish.

With the power of Mitanni vanquished, the states of Syria fell to him one after the other. Suppiluliumas lists them as Aleppo, Mukish, Niya, Arakhtu, Qatna and Nuhashshe (*see* Map 3). Egypt had also seen slip from her control the great trading city of Ugarit and the vital strategic possession of Qadesh. That this could occur without any military response by the Nilotic kingdom is worthy of some consideration. The failure of Pharaoh to come to the aid of his erstwhile ally is often cited as evidence of the disinterestedness of Amenophis IV (hereinafter Akhenaten) in his Asiatic empire. From the vantage-point of El Amarna, however, matters were not perceived in that way. Notwithstanding her treaty obligations the early years of Akhenaten's reign had seen a cooling of relations with Mitanni. It mattered little to Egypt who occupied northern Syria as long as the borders with the Nilotic kingdom were respected. On that matter it would seem that the wily Hittite monarch had made clear beforehand that his campaign was directed solely against Mitanni and its Syrian dependencies.

Indeed, the Hittite occupation of Qadesh had not been intended but followed upon the unilateral attempt by the king of Qadesh, operating as he believed in the interests of his Egyptian overlord, to block the Hittite advance southwards. Having been defeated in battle and the city taken, the leading men of Qadesh, including its king and his son Aitakama, had been carried off to Hattusas. A significant possession now lay in Hittite hands and its retention or otherwise would be regarded by Egypt as the litmus test of Hatti's true intentions. The return of Aitakama seemed to demonstrate the veracity of the Hittite claim to have no design on Egyptian territory, particularly as he was able to renew Qadesh' status as a vassal of Egypt. Within a short time of his being installed as ruler of Qadesh, however, Aitakama began to act in a manner that suggests he may well have become a stooge of the Hittites. Rulers of other Egyptian vassal cities reported attempts by the ruler of Qadesh to subvert them to the Hittite cause, and attacks by Qadesh on Egyptian vassals in Upe suggest that he was functioning as a Trojan Horse against the Egyptians on behalf of Hatti.

Unwilling as ever to intervene, Egypt turned to Aziru, the ruler of Amurru, and charged him to protect Egyptian interests in the region. But, as in the days of his father, Aziru exploited the Egyptian commission and gold for his own ends and once again began to expand Amurru's boundaries at the expense of neighbouring vassal states. Word also reached Egypt of disturbing rumours that Aziru was playing a double game by flirting with the Hittites and had even entertained envoys of the Anatolian power. With Qadesh almost certainly tacitly in the Hittite camp and Amurru in contact with the Hittites, the time had now come for Egypt to act. Aziru was ordered to present himself at the court of Pharaoh to explain his behaviour while that of Qadesh was interpreted as a vassal in revolt. A military solution was necessary. Although very sparsely documented, an Egyptian assault on Qadesh in the reign of Akhenaten is now assumed to have occurred and failed. Qadesh now passed into the domain of the Hittite monarch, its recovery becoming the focus of Egyptian military efforts down until the time of Rameses II. Aziru reluctantly journeyed to the court of Akhenaten where his enforced stay lasted several years. It was the continued reluctance of the Egyptians to base strong military forces in Syria and their perseverance in maintaining the policy of ruling through proxies that determined them to release Aziru and return him to Amurru. The presumption was that he was at least trustworthy to the extent that the interests of Amurru coincided with those of Egypt.

In the meantime Suppiluliumas had undertaken a major reorganization of the Hittite position in northern Syria. Carchemish had finally fallen and the Hittite king proceeded to place that city and Aleppo under the direct rule of his sons. With their own military establishments they would be available to encourage the loyalty of the vassals and counter any potential trouble. The proximity of such large nominally 'Hittite' forces in Syria but the absence of any Egyptian equivalent in her own Syrian territories dramatically changed the perceived balance of

◀ *During the period from 1352 to 1318 three generals wore the double crown of Upper and Lower Egypt. The most important of these and the last king of the 18th Dynasty was Horemheb. He was a stern ruler who set about the internal reorganization of the kingdom and strengthened the lines of communications with Asia.*

power in the region. For Aziru the presence of a powerful Hittite power base in northern Syria determined where his loyalties would now lie. Having returned to Amurru he revoked his vassal oath to Egypt and '... fell at the feet of the Sun, the Great king of Hatti' and thus became a vassal of Suppiluliumas.

With the defection of Amurru and Qadesh Egypt had lost two vital strategic possessions in central Syria and the border with Hatti had now been thrust south of the Eleutheros valley. That the Hittites came to view these new borders as permanent was a perception never shared by Egypt and indeed the recovery of the lost lands of Amurru, Qadesh and beyond was to become the avowed ambition of the early pharaohs of the 19th Dynasty.

The Campaigns of Seti I

With the demise of Tutankhamun in 1352 the army seized the reins of power in Egypt and over the next thirty-two years the throne of the two lands was occupied by three generals. Any desire to recover Amurru and Qadesh were set aside in the face of the need to reorganize Egypt after the troubles of the reign of Akhenaten. This notwithstanding, it is clear that in the wake of the loss of these possessions Egyptian policy towards its 'empire' underwent a major shift. The use of proxies as a substitute for military power had clearly been found wanting. Its replacement by a new policy described by Egyptologists as 'military occupation' finds testimony in the archaeological record in the late Amarna period and early 19th Dynasty. The inference to be drawn is that the army now became the guiding hand in the formulation of policy in Asia. As early as the reign of Horemheb (1348-20) it is possible to discern the will to recover Egypt's 'lost territories' by military means. It was he who began the resettlement of the old Hyksos capital at Avaris in the eastern delta. Its nearness to the routes to Canaan and Syria made it an excellent site as a forward operating base for the rapid transit of Egyptian forces to Asia; indeed it was to become such under Seti and his son.

It was with the accession of Seti I to the throne of Egypt that intention became translated into reality. There was no ambiguity to the new Pharaoh's ambition and it was writ large in his selection of his Horus name. In a conscious allusion to the praenomen of Amosis I, founder of the 18th Dynasty and Egypt's empire in Asia, he called himself 'Repeater of Birth', that is, inaugurator of a new beginning of Egypt's greatness. In the first year of his reign Seti took his army into Palestine to destroy a coalition of hostile Canaanite princes and thence northwards along the coast into the Lebanon. The importance of this campaign lay not so much in what it achieved as in how it was at once a pointer to the future and a conscious allusion to the past. For the first time, possibly, since the reign of Tuthmosis IV Pharaoh was personally leading the army into Egypt's Asiatic possessions. This served notice that a break had been made with the policy of the Amarna period when the military had been employed in penny packets in essentially police actions. Now

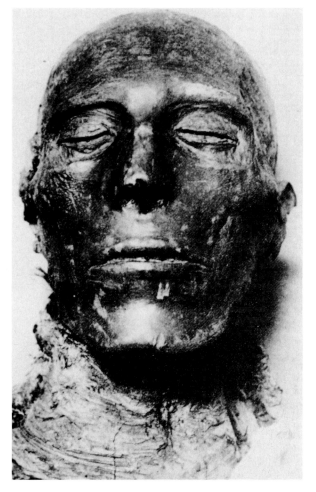

▲ *The mummified features of Seti I (1318-04) still manage to convey the determination and resolve that lay behind his vigorous and successful campaigns to recover Qadesh from the Hittites. Nevertheless, the very fact that his son Rameses II set out to retake the city means that the Hittites had possibly successfully reclaimed it even before Seti's death.*

Egyptian interests would be served by the full army and led by Pharaoh in person. For Seti, as indeed for his son, the model for their policy in Asia was Tuthmosis III, and in a conscious emulation of his strategy Seti led his armies sometime after Year 2 northwards to begin his offensive against the Hittite empire.

Seti's Syrian campaigns are recorded on the west wing of his war monument at Karnak. Attending the visual register is the statement, '... The ascent that Pharaoh ... made in order to destroy the land of Qadesh and the land of Amurru'. A fragment of a

victory stela recovered from Qadesh and bearing Seti's name is testimony to his seizure of the city as it passed under Egypt's aegis for the last time. Amurru, however, is thought at this stage to have remained true to its Hatti allegiance. Possession of Qadesh, however, allowed Pharaoh to realize the Hittites' greatest fear. Emulating Tuthmosis III, he took his armies into northern Syria by way of Qadesh and there met and defeated a Hittite force. That the Hittite response to this was not more overwhelming given the high stakes involved has led some scholars to argue that the bulk of the main Hittite army, and not the Syrian vassal levies Seti actually defeated, were heavily involved elsewhere. And indeed, the problem posed by Assyria on Hatti's eastern borders may well have meant that in the short term the Egyptian success in Syria would have to be tolerated.

None the less it would seem that before Seti's death in 1304 Qadesh had already returned to the Hittite fold because in the annals of Mursilis there is a suggestion of the conclusion of a treaty with Egypt which presumably returned affairs in Syria to the status quo ante.

So matters rested. It was not until the fourth year of the reign of Seti's son Rameses II that the peace in Syria was once more shattered when seemingly out of the blue Amurru, playing its game of old, defected to Egypt. In that same year Pharaoh led his armies northward in a fast dash to receive, in all probability, the formal oath of submission from Benteshina, King of Amurru. The new Hittite monarch Muwatallish was not oblivious to the aspirations of his Egyptian counterpart. Rameses was known to harbour great ambitions in northern Syria, but to realize these Egypt would first need to secure Qadesh. In this matter Hatti had to act. Should Qadesh also fall the Hittite position in northern Syria, and in particular the strategic satellite states of Aleppo and Carchemish, would be under threat from Egypt. Unlike the situation in the days of his father, there was no immediate Assyrian threat to distract the Hittite monarch.

So it was that in the winter of 1301 Muwatallish set about organizing an army that would, he intended, recover Amurru, secure Qadesh and shatter totally Egypt's military pretensions in the region. The venue for the coming contest was not in doubt in either camp. Beneath the walls of Qadesh Rameses and Muwatallish would fight in one of the great battles of history to settle by trial of arms the future of their respective empires in Syria.

◀ *A graphic based on the battle reliefs of Seti I at Karnak which shows the Egyptian army fighting on the plain before Qadesh. Of particular note is the shape of the citadel in the top right of the register and below that the vegetation that marks the line of the tributary of the Orontes known as Al-Mukadiyah to the west of the city.*

▶ *It was in early June of 1304 that Rameses II ascended the throne of Egypt as sole ruler of the Kingdom of the Two Lands. This black granite statue of the Pharaoh shows him as he appeared about the time of the battle of Qadesh when he would have been in his mid to late twenties. He is shown wearing the 'blue' or 'war' crown known as the Khepresh which was worn in battle.*

◀ *Rameses II was the greatest of the pharaonic builders of ancient Egypt. Few of his monuments are more impressive than the great temple at Abu Simbel. Visible expression of the deification of the Pharaoh in his lifetime, it is the foremost example of the numerous buildings that litter the two lands bearing his name.*

▼▶ *The presumed mummy of Rameses II, discovered among a large cache bearing the names of some of the most illustrious rulers of Ancient Egypt, by Emil Brugsch-Bey in the Valley of the Kings in 1881. Recent medical analysis in the 1967 mummy survey, however, suggests it may be that of a man in the middle to late fifties, whereas Rameses II was in his 90th year when he died.*

RAMESES II AND MUWATALLISH

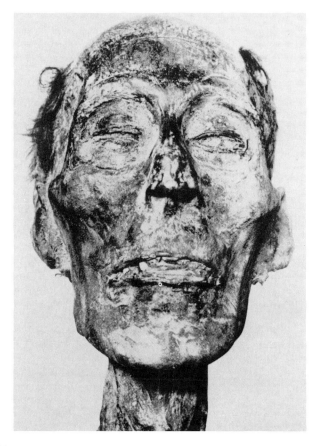

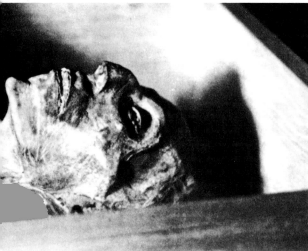

In the light of the avowed intention of the early 19th Dynasty Pharaohs to recover Egypt's 'lost' lands in Syria, the initial success of Seti I in recovering Qadesh and subsequently losing it again by treaty must have been irksome to the young Rameses. As crown prince he had been schooled from an early age in the ways of the camp and had participated in his father's Libyan and Syrian campaigns. So when his father died unexpectedly in the summer of 1304 he ascended the throne of the two lands imbued with the desire to gain the glory of their recovery for himself.

He was in his mid twenties when the twin crown of Egypt was placed upon his head and his official title announced as: 'Rameses II, Falcon King, He of the Two Goddesses, Horus of Gold, King of Upper and Lower Egypt, Use-mare, Son of Re'. As master of one of the world's great empires, confident and certain of his destiny, it was only a matter of time before the new Pharaoh would set out on the road to Asia to settle once and for all the ownership of Syria.

It is apparent that the pharaonic ambition did not perceive as any hindrance the legal nicety of the treaty concluded with Hatti by his father. For Rameses the vista of possibilities did not end with Qadesh and Amurru but extended beyond to emulating the achievements of the great warrior Pharaohs of the previous dynasty. Although some three years were to elapse before Amurru's defection precipitated the war with Hatti, it is clear that Rameses had been making preparations for its inevitable outbreak for some time. Apart from changes to and careful cultivation of the army, the rebuilding of the old Hyksos capital Avaris, now renamed Pi-Rameses and transformed into a major base for military operations in Asia, served as a major indicator of pharaonic intentions.

Of his counterpart on the Hittite throne we know much less. Muwatallish was the second of the four children of Mursilis II, the opponent of Seti in his Syrian wars. The death of his elder brother brought Muwatallish to the throne of Hatti some four years before Rameses was crowned king in Egypt. He was undoubtedly a strong and able ruler and a man of no mean intelligence. His reorganization of Hatti's western empire released the forces that allowed him to field against Rameses at Qadesh the largest army ever raised by the Hittite empire. That he was absolutely determined to trounce once and for all Egyptian pretensions to resurrect their northern Syrian territories cannot be doubted, and is nowhere better seen than in the petitional prayer that Muwatallish offered to his gods:

'On which campaign My Majesty shall march, then if you O Gods, support me and I conquer the land of Amurru — whether I overcome it by force of arms, or whether it makes peace with me — and I seize the king of Amurru, then ... I will richly reward you, O Gods...!'

◄ *On the first and second pylons of the mortuary temple of Rameses II, nowadays known as The Rameseum, are reliefs depicting the Battle of Qadesh. The building itself was on a colossal scale. The building was wrongly described by Diodorus as 'the tomb of Osymandyas'. This error arose from a misuse of Use-mare, part of the praenomen of the Pharaoh. It was, however, this name and an image of the fallen colossus of Rameses at the Rameseum that vaguely inspired Shelley to pen his famous sonnet 'Ozymandias'.*

THE OPPOSING ARMIES

The Might of Hatti

The army raised by the King of Hatti to challenge the resurgent Egyptian empire and its new Pharaoh at Qadesh was drawn from all corners of the Hittite empire. The successful campaigns fought by Muwatallish against the restive and troublesome kingdoms of western and northern Anatolia and their consequent re-organization allowed him to draw on a very large body of troops for his Syrian war against Egypt. At the heart of this army, composed of allied and vassal forces, was that of Great Hatti itself.

In common with Late Bronze Age armies that of Hatti was built around the chariot and infantry. The former existed in the form of a small standing force which was rapidly expanded in the campaigning season when men would be called to the colours in fulfilment of the feudal obligations to the king. As in Egypt the chariotry tended to attract men from the landed nobility and was an arm of high status. Indeed, the expense of maintaining a chariot and teams was also part of the feudal obligation of a landed noble to his Lord. It is clear that the Hittites quite happily employed mercenary troops and in the Rameside Poem describing the Qadesh campaign Pharaoh alludes to this when he says: '... He had no silver left in his land, he stripped it of all its possessions and gave them to all the foreign countries in order to bring them with him to fight.' While making allowances for pharaonic hyperbole it is most certain that a great deal of wealth was expended by Muwatallish to raise his army to the numbers deemed necessary to realize his campaign aims. It was for this reason that many Hittite soldiers forwent pay, the prospect of booty being held as an incentive to fight well. Clearly such a policy held dangers. As we shall see, it was the lure of the booty of the camp of Amun and Pharaoh's enclosure that drew the Hittite charioteers into premature combat.

In contradistinction to that of its great southern enemy, the principal offensive arm of the Hittite army was the chariot. The difference extended to its tactical employment which, being predicated on different assumptions, was revealed most clearly in the design and crewing of the chariot itself. Although Hittite chariot crews did employ the composite bow it never supplanted the predominant weapon, the long, thrusting spear. The Hittites viewed the chariot as essentially an assault weapon designed to crash into and break up groups of enemy infantry. With its axle placed centrally and strong enough to carry a three-man crew, it was somewhat slower and certainly less manoeuvrable than its Egyptian counterpart. Each design had its respective advantages and disadvantages. When employed in optimum conditions the shock tactics of Hittite chariotry would open the way for their infantry to follow through and finish off the enemy. It followed that the latter arm played a secondary role to that of the chariotry.

Unlike the Egyptian infantry, who operated in country relatively uniform in terms of terrain and temperature — as reflected in the relative sameness of their dress, Hittite infantry fought in more diverse physical conditions. As such their dress tends to reflect the needs of the campaign. Certainly those illustrated on the Qadesh reliefs cannot be taken as indicative of the standard appearance. The long white coverall worn by so many at Qadesh is not reflected in the dress of the infantryman at the Kings Gate at Hattusas. The weaponry of the Hittite footsoldier was in many ways similar to his Egyptian counterpart. The 'thr' warriors surrounding Muwatallish at Qadesh are armed with a long thrusting spear and short stabbing daggers similar to those carried by the chariotry. Although iron weaponry had begun to make its appearance in the Hittite army by this time, the major hand weapons were the bronze sickle sword and the bronze battle-axe. While it is clear that Hittite soldiers did wear

The Hittite Empire and its Allies at Qadesh, 1300 BC

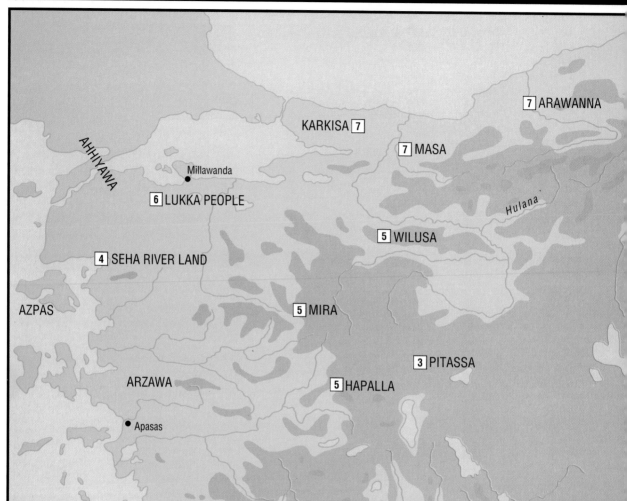

7 ARAWANNA

KARKISA 7

7 MASA

AHHIYAWA

Millawanda

6 LUKKA PEOPLE

Hulana

5 WILUSA

4 SEHA RIVER LAND

AZPAS

5 MIRA

3 PITASSA

ARZAWA

5 HAPALLA

Apasas

Tarhuntassa

Mediterranean

ALASIYA

	HATTI & ALLIES	KNOWN LEADERS	APPROXIMATE NUMBERS
1	Hatti	Muwatallish; Hattushilish	500 chariots; 5,000 infantry
2	Hakpis	Hattushilish	500 chariots; 5,000 infantry
3	Pitassa	Mitannamuwash	500 chariots; 5,000 infantry
4	Seha River Land	Masturish	100 chariots; 1,000 infantry
5	Wilusa, Mira & Hapalla	Piyama-Inarash (?)	500 chariots; 5,000 infantry
6	Lukka People	?	100 chariots; 2,000 infantry
7	Masa, Karkisa & Arawanna	?	200 chariots; 4,000 infantry
8	Kizzuwadna	?	200 chariots; 2,000 infantry
9	Carchemish	Sahurunuwash	200 chariots; 2,000 infantry
10	Mitanni	Sattuara	200 chariots; 2,000 infantry
11	Ugarit	Niqmepa	200 chariots; 2,000 infantry
12	Aleppo	Talmi-Sarruma	200 chariots; 2,000 infantry
13	Nuhashshe	?	100 chariots; 1,000 infantry
14	Kinza (Qadesh)	Niqmaddu	200 chariots; 2,000 infantry
Total:	18 Allied and Vassal States		3,700 chariots; 40,000 infantry

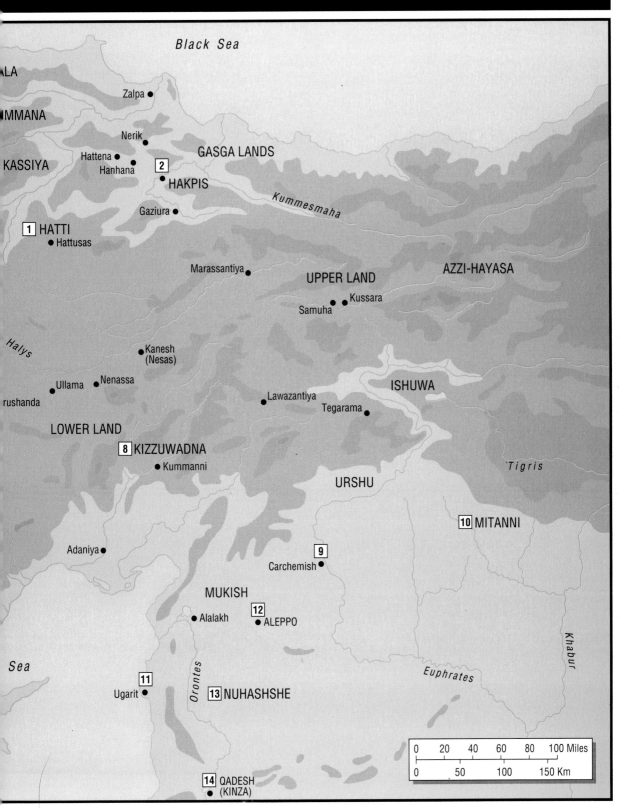

Black Sea

LA

MMANA

KASSIYA

Zalpa ●

Nerik ●

Hattena ● Hanhana ● ● 2 ● HAKPIS

GASGA LANDS

Kummesmaha

Gaziura ●

1 HATTI
● Hattusas

Marassantiya ●

UPPER LAND

AZZI-HAYASA

● Kussara
Samuha ●

Halys

● Kanesh
(Nesas)

● Ullama ● Nenassa

rushanda

LOWER LAND

Lawazantiya ●
Tegarama ●

ISHUWA

8 KIZZUWADNA
● Kummanni

URSHU

Tigris

10 MITANNI

Adaniya ●

9
Carchemish ●

MUKISH

12
● Alalakh ● ALEPPO

Sea

Khabur

Orontes

11
Ugarit ●

13 NUHASHSHE

Euphrates

0	20	40	60	80	100 Miles
0		50	100		150 Km

14 QADESH
● (KINZA)

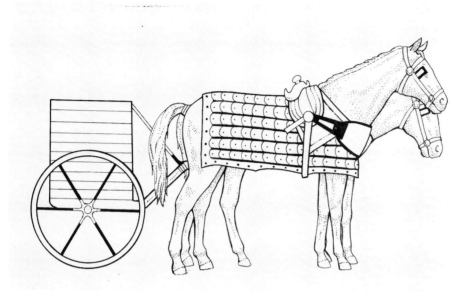

when they were vulnera-
ble to the effective
archery of the Egyptians.
The destruction of large
numbers of Hittite chari-
ots by their Egyptian
counterparts suggests that
with momentum and sur-
prise lost Hittite chariots
were very vulnerable to
the type of tactics
employed by Rameses
and his chariotry on the
day.

▼A section from the
Rameseum reliefs show-
ing Hittite chariots at
Qadesh. These have actu-
ally been recut; originally
they illustrated Egyptian
chariots with the wheels
to the rear of the cab. The
traditional three-man
crew has been added with
the distinctive Hittite
shield held prominently
forward by the bearer to
protect the other men as
the vehicles charge..

▲ Our best source for the
appearance of Hittite
chariots are the Egyptian
reliefs of the battle of
Qadesh. It is clear from a
number of sources that
Hittite chariot design and
tactics were predicated on
different assumptions
from those of their great
southern enemy. The
effectiveness of their
chariot arm lay in its
value as an assault
weapon, where the sheer
weight of the vehicle en
masse and at the charge
was employed to crash
into and demolish lines of
enemy infantry. This is
also reflected in the fact
that the principal weapon
carried was the long stabbing spear that armed the
three crewmen, driver,
spearman and shield-
bearer. In order to accommodate this heavier load
the axle of the Hittite
vehicle was mid cab
which frequently led to
vehicles overturning at
speed because they were
less stable than their
Egyptian counterpart.
Given the lesser manoeu-
vrability of the Hittite
machine, it was an 'easi-
er' target for Egyptian
archers, whether mounted
or on foot. It was neces-
sary therefore for the
spearman to be protected
by the shield-bearer par-
ticularly in the charge

helmets and bronze scale armour, many of those in the Qadesh reliefs are shown without either. It has been suggested that the 'white' coverall, employed when on campaign in Syria, may have been worn over the scale armour used by many troops.

There can be no doubting that the Hittites were masters of strategy and were prepared and able to use guile and sleight of hand if it would yield advantage. Evidence suggests that where possible the Hittites would so engineer a situation as to catch their opponents in open battle where the chariotry could be used to greatest advantage, and in such a way as to allow the infantry to follow through and deliver the *coup de grâce*. Indeed, this view of their operations on the battlefield is held by the author to justify the case that what transpired at Qadesh was not

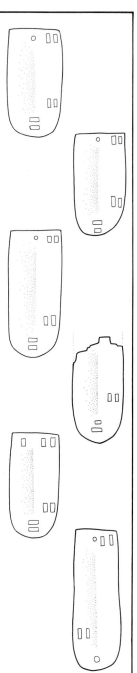

◀ *There are very few sources illustrating the appearance of Hittite warriors. The most famous is from the left-hand inner side of the King's Gate at Bogazkoy, the modern name for the site of the ancient Hittite capital Hattusas. He is armed with a curved pointed sword and a four-pronged and socketed battleaxe. His helmet is probably of bronze with flaps to cover the neck and cheeks and is decorated with a long plume which hangs down his back.*

◀ *These fragments of scale armour recovered from the Hittite capital Hattusas are, like their Egyptian counterparts, of bronze. Fragments of iron scales have been found, but it is extremely unlikely that at the time of the battle any iron scale armour would have been employed. Clearly shown are the holes through which the scales would have been fixed to the skirt. In the reliefs many of the crew of Hittite chariots are illustrated wearing such armour.*

the battle the Hittites had intended to fight, but that they were in fact awaiting the arrival and concentration of the entire Egyptian army on Qadesh before deploying and forcing the battle on the plain.

The Hittites were a truly formidable military foe and while Rameses could condescendingly and pejoratively speak of them as 'effeminate ones' by virtue of their predilection for wearing their hair long, he was to learn very quickly that the warriors

of Hatti were every bit as brave and formidable as any that the Nilotic empire could field.

It is contended in a number of places in this text that Hatti and Egypt had agreed to Qadesh as the venue for the battle to resolve their respective claims to Syria. In part this assertion arises from the important role Law played in the Hittite dealings with all aspects of its empire. With the defection of Amurru in the winter of 1302/01, the view from

◄ *Hittite chariot and crew. It is clear that, notwithstanding Rameses' disparaging reference to the Hittites as 'effeminate ones' by virtue of their tendency to be clean-shaven and wear their hair long, they were formidable soldiers. Their most powerful arm was the chariotry, and the example shown here typifies the features of the Hittite vehicle. The three-man crew comprised the unarmoured driver, and armoured spearman and the shield carrier, who provided protection for the spearman. The design and armament of the Hittite chariot was optimised for its primary purpose of close-order combat.*

ing charged Rameses with inspiring the defection of his vassal, Amurru, the Hittite king would have told Rameses that the matter between them was now to be settled by the judgement of the gods and in the theatre of war. Sometime during the early winter of 1301 it is very likely that a Hittite messenger arrived at the court of Pharaoh at Pi-Rameses with a formal message from Muwatallish. In its essence and sentiment its wording would have differed not at all from that sent to the King of Arzawa some years before by his father Mursilis:

'My subjects who went over to you, when I demanded them back from you, you did not restore then to me: and you called me a child and made light of me. Up then! Let us fight, and let the Storm-god, my lord, decide our case!'

As the to venue for their contest? It would be Qadesh, for as we shall see, there could be none other!

Pharaoh, Army and State

It was on Day 9 of the second month of the summer season (mid to late April 1300) that the Egyptian army, having been mustered at the Delta city and military outpost of Pi-Rameses, advanced beyond the great frontier fortress of Tjel and on to the coast road to Gaza, to begin the month-long trek to its appointed battlefield beneath the walls of Qadesh in central Syria. For Rameses II, in the van of this great host, imbued with the burning desire to restore his empire's northern borders and emulate the martial exploits of his illustrious pharaonic forebears, the prospect of victory over the Hittites must have seemed inevitable. Such optimistic expectations, shared by king and rank and file alike, were surely not misplaced, for this army was one of the largest and best equipped that had yet been assembled for offensive operations by the Egyptian state. With its mass chariot squadrons, infantry companies, glittering Standards and military musicians, the Rameside army was the heir to and the ultimate expression of an Egyptian military tradition already some three centuries old.

Although Egypt had always maintained military forces in the Old and Middle Kingdoms, the particular form that emerged in the New Kingdom and the manner in which the state became organized to

Hatti was that the treaty ratified by Seti and Mursilis guaranteeing the borders of the two empires in Syria had been broken. It is known that the Hittite kings took great care to justify a declaration of war. Certainly the defection of Amurru constituted in the strict legal sense a *casus belli*. Although no mention is derivable from Hittite or Egyptian records, it seems very likely that Muwatallish took the necessary legal steps prior to his declaration of war. Hav-

serve its needs dates from the mid 16th century. In the wake of the defeat of the Hyksos by Amosis I, the first Pharaoh of the 18th Dynasty and New Kingdom, Egypt's policy towards those states and peoples beyond her eastern frontiers fundamentally changed. Inheriting the mantle of the Hyksos, Egypt now found herself as tacit overlord of territories stretching as far north as the River Euphrates. The emergence of a recognizably imperial policy towards Canaan and the Levant coincided with the realization that the projection of military power far beyond Egypt's eastern frontier was the most effective method for ensuring her defence. Such now

became the keystone of Egypt's policy in dealing with the Levant and goes far to explain her involvement there over the next four centuries. The corollary of such a policy was the existence of a professional standing army equipped with the full panoply of weaponry consistent with Late Bronze Age chariot warfare, and a state organized for supporting such on a large scale. In the period of economic reconstruction and political centralization that followed the defeat of the Hyksos, the foundations of the Egyptian military state, able to sustain a powerful standing army and a wide-ranging imperial policy in Canaan and beyond, were laid. In a very real

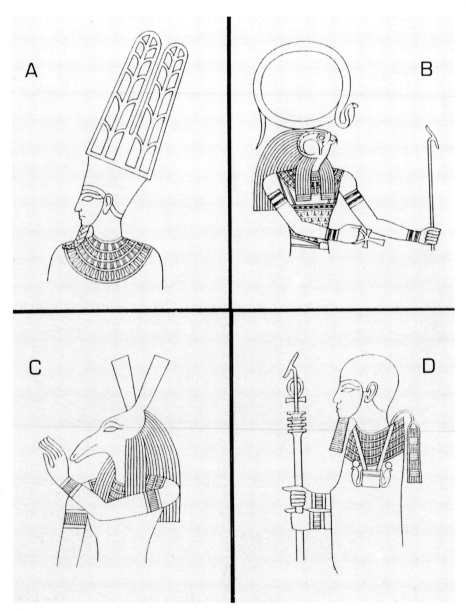

◀ Each of the four corps of the Egyptian army deployed in the Qadesh campaign was organized around troops from a specific region or temple estate in Egypt and named for the local god. The premier corps was that of Amun, the god of Thebes ('A'). The second ('B') was that of P'Re (The Re), the sun god of Heliopolis. These two corps were the original units of the army to which were added that of Sutekh or Set ('C'). Sutekh was regarded as the Lord of Upper Egypt and was particularly venerated by the pharaohs of the 19th Dynasty. Seti I was named for Sutekh. The corps of Sutekh was based on Avaris, later Pi-Rameses in the eastern delta. Ptah ('D') was raised by Rameses II and was named for the local god of Memphis. It must be said, however, that Ptah may have been raised before the corps of Sutekh although Seti I does not mention the corps of Ptah in his campaign of Year 1 in Canaan when only Amun, P'Re and Sutekh (Set) are spoken of.

sense it was this translation of Egypt into a military state, with all that presaged on the international scene in the Ancient Near East, that is the dominating, if not defining, feature of what is called the 'New Kingdom' period of her history.

The emergence of the professional military as a distinct caste during the New Kingdom had a major impact on the internal politics of the Egyptian state. Not the least of factors contributing to the growth of influence of the military was the relationship of many of the 18th and 19th Dynasty pharaohs with their army. Schooled from an early age in discipline and the arts of war, the heir to the throne was entrusted to officers charged with imparting the knowledge, skills and understanding required by a martial ruler. Such conditioning was subsequently apparent in the manner that as pharaoh, Egypt and the empire were governed. The archetype of the military king was Tuthmosis III (1504–1450) who by his military exploits raised the status of Egypt to that of the greatest power in the ancient Near East (and whose example was to spur the military ambitions of Rameses II) and honed the Egyptian army into the most formidable instrument of war the world had yet seen.

The influence and power of the military in the government of Egypt grew during the 18th Dynasty and had become openly manifest by the early 19th Dynasty. Whether serving as staff officers with direct access to the court or in 'retirement' and rewarded by appointment as personal attendants, stewards of the royal estates or tutors to the pharaoh's children, the military came to play a formative role in the life of the state. So great had this influence become that during the reign of boy-Pharaoh Tutankhamun (c.1352) it was the military who controlled the reins of government. With the death of Ay the throne passed into the hands of the army strongman Horemheb who vigorously set about the internal reorganization of the kingdom following the depredations of the reign of Akhenaten. This was but the prelude to what was intended to be the revival of Egypt's Asian empire and recovery of the lands lost to the Hittites under Suppiluliumas. With his death, the torch was passed on to his successor and the founder of the 19th Dynasty, Rameses I, Seti I and in turn to Rameses II. The new 19th Dynasty had its roots in the military and

under their aegis the army was highly influential.

The sociological impact of the army on Egyptian life in the New Kingdom was significant and can be gauged by the manner in which it came to be seen as a means of social and material advancement for rich and poor alike. For the latter, service with the army opened up the prospect of the acquisition of wealth and status unimaginable to the peasant who stayed on the land. To one who demonstrated bravery and intelligence not only was there the prospect of reward of the 'Gold of Valour' and a share in the rich booty taken on campaign, but also the possibility of promotion to officer rank. Other benefits

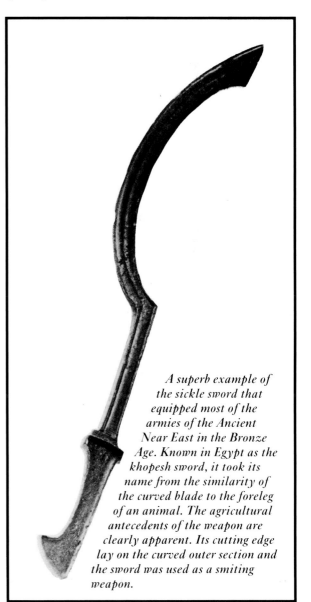

A superb example of the sickle sword that equipped most of the armies of the Ancient Near East in the Bronze Age. Known in Egypt as the khopesh sword, it took its name from the similarity of the curved blade to the foreleg of an animal. The agricultural antecedents of the weapon are clearly apparent. Its cutting edge lay on the curved outer section and the sword was used as a smiting weapon.

accruing from successful service illustrate the concern taken by the pharaohs to care and nurture the soldiery as a professional caste. A late Rameside papyrus details the granting of land for farms by pharaoh to officers, charioteers, mercenaries as well as simple rankers. In addition pharaoh would provide the beneficiary with cattle and servants from the royal household for employment on these farms. Although the beneficiary paid taxes on their employment, the recipient was able to retain them as long as one of the male members of his family, in direct line of succession, was available to serve in the army or navy. It was this policy more than any other that helps explain the increasingly hereditary nature of the military in the late 18th and 19th Dynasties. An earlier taxation papyrus dating from the third year of Seti I's reign (c.1315) lists the householders of a district in the city of Memphis and serves to demonstrate the standing of the military in Egyptian society. Alongside those of civilian occupations are listed an army scribe, marines, marine standard-bearers, charioteers, battalion commanders, a captain and a lieutenant-general.

The high status and wealth of the army and the manner in which it was seemingly 'indulged' by the pharaohs brought forth the ire of other professions who saw able recruits 'seduced' away from the more traditional routes to social advancement. This is nowhere better illustrated than in the diatribes against the lures of the military life offered by scribes in 20th-Dynasty sources. The self-serving invective of the scribes failed completely to perceive that the relationship of pharaoh to his army was not one of indulgence but pragmatic self-interest. The pharaohs of the 18th and 19th Dynasties assumed that reciprocity in the care for their soldiery would be shown by the military on the field of battle. Obligation demanded that each soldier strive to 'win a good name' and by bravery and hard fighting deliver to pharaoh the victories in war that were his due. Such observations offer important insights for our understanding of the events at Qadesh.

Indeed, it is the perceived failure of the troops of Amun and P'Re at Qadesh to hold their ground and face the Hittite chariotry that results in Rameses bitterly denouncing them for desertion and cowardice. The vehemence with which he pours scorn on the survivors of the two divisions after the battle

makes clear his conviction that the troops had broken the compact with their Lord and in abandoning the field of battle had committed the capital offence of treason consequentially translating their status from that of subject to rebel. The author of the 'Poem' has Rameses speaking thus:

'How cowardly are your hearts, my chariotry, nor is there any worthy of trust among you any longer. Is there not one among you to whom I did a good deed in my land? Did not I arise as Lord when you were poor, and I caused you to be high officers by my Beneficence every day, placing the son over the possessions of his father, and making to cease all evil that was in this land? And I released unto you your servants and gave you others who had been taken from you. Whoever asked petitions "I will do it" said I to him, every day. Never had a Lord done for them for his army, those things which my Majesty did for your sakes. The crime which my infantry and my chariotry have done is greater than can be told.'

As we shall see in our consideration of the aftermath of the battle, what has been interpreted by some commentators as a continuation of the battle into a second day, may be more credibly explained as pharaoh visiting summary judgement on numbers of his own 'cowardly' soldiers whom he adjudged to be 'rebellious' subjects.

The Rameside Army

It was in all probability during the short reign of his father Rameses I, that crown prince Seti began the task of enlarging the Egyptian army. The imperative to do so arose from the new dynasty's self-appointed task of recovering Egypt's lost lands in central Syria. Such an ambition, by its very nature, could only be realized by force of arms — and in the kingdom of Hatti the new dynasty faced a formidable foe.

Although we possess very little information about the gathering of military intelligence in ancient Egypt it seems reasonable to assume that the state, as did other powers of the time, made some effort to discern the military potential of rival kingdoms. In the light of this assumption, the expansion of the Egyptian army is understandable, for the Hittite kingdom had displayed its ability to field large and highly effective armies on many occasions. Certainly the military activities of the Hittites during the preceding century had done much to broadcast the formidable nature of their power. In consequence Seti was under no illusion as to the magnitude of the military task that faced him. To reinvigorate Egypt's empire and successfully wrest the territories of central Syria from Hatti would require a major effort in equipping and fielding an army far larger than any raised by Egypt before.

▶ *Egyptian heavy infantryman. Throughout the New Kingdom, the Egyptian army was built around a core of long-service veteran heavy infantry, as shown here. While this grizzled and battle-hardened 'menfyt' carries the same weaponry of bronze khopesh sword and spear that typified most New Kingdom infantry, his appearance is that of a 19th Dynasty trooper and thus represents the heavy infantry found in four corps of Amun, P'Re, Sutekh (Set) and Ptah at the Battle of Qadesh. Distinctive 19th Dynasty features include the strengthened headdress, the stiffened linen-padded body armour and large oval-shaped groin guard. (Angus McBride)*

The Field Army

The expansion was most obviously discernible in the addition of two additional army corps to the field army. It had ever been the tradition for Egyptian soldiers to march and fight in local contingents. In the New Kingdom these were organized as self-contained corps which, when fully assembled for campaign, numbered approximately 5,000 men. Although a broken passage in the annals of Tuthmosis III suggests that his army may have been organized into four corps during the Battle of Megiddo, only two are actually mentioned at a later date in an edict of Horemheb. A third, Sutekh (Set), was raised either in the reign of Rameses I or by Seti, with the fourth very early in the reign of his son, Rameses II. Each corps was based upon a temple or estate region in Egypt and named in honour of the local god. That of Amun was from Thebes with P'Re from Heliopolis and Sutekh raised from men of the north-east delta and was based upon the old Hyksos capital at Avaris. The fourth, named for the god Ptah, was drawn from the Memphite region. It was these four corps that composed the bulk of the Egyptian forces deployed for the Qadesh campaign.

It is interesting to note how a number of commentators have perceived Rameses' decision to advance his army on Qadesh in four corps as an aberration on his part. Such a view serves to allow them

▲ Although dating from the 15th century this Theban tomb painting shows the technique of manufacturing shields which had changed little if at all some two centuries later. Having scraped the hide, it is then shaped to fit the wooden frame. Finished shields can be seen to the rear of the figure in the upper centre of the picture. The hides of cows were used for ordinary ranks, whereas the shields of royal persons were made from the hides of more exotic animals.

severely to criticize him and argue that it was this 'decision' to 'divide' his army that opened the way for the Hittites to attack his strung-out forces, bringing them to the verge of catastrophic defeat. The criticism is not valid for it is quite clear that the advance of the army on Qadesh in four corps was not an idiosyncratic whim on the part of Rameses but totally consistent with standard Egyptian military practice. There were indeed sound strategic and logistical reasons for why this was the case.

The deliberately self-contained nature of each corps, comprising approximately 5,000 men of whom some 4,000 were infantry with the other 1,000 crewing the 500 attached chariots, provided the Pharaoh with a remarkable degree of flexibility on campaign. Locally dispersed operations in which each corps could be allocated separate objectives were balanced by the manner in which each operated within supporting distance, although it is clear that they could operate independently at some distance from one another when needs demanded. One of the best examples of this practice, apart from that of Qadesh itself, dates from the first campaign of Seti in northern Palestine in about 1318. In order to destroy a coalition of Asiatic princes, '... his majesty sent the first army of Amun, named "Mighty of Bows", to the town of Hamath, the first army of P'Re, named "Plentiful of Valour", to the town of Beth Shan, and the first army of Set, named "Strong of Bows" to the town of Yenoam.' A well-balanced fighting force of infantry, archers and chariots was more than adequate to deal on a piece-meal basis with a nascent coalition of Palestinian princes. Indeed this description of an armed excursion is more characteristic of the bulk of Egyptian military operations in the New Kingdom period than ever was the full-scale battle such as Megiddo or Qadesh. While on the one hand the corps structure of the Egyptian army conveyed great tactical flexibility, it was also a sound and rational response to the difficulties of supplying and feeding large numbers of soldiers during this period. Consideration of this issue will also provide insight into matters of some import for understanding how events unfolded at Qadesh.

Although the Egyptian army possessed a well-organized commissariat, the feeding of a large expeditionary force on the move through Canaan and northwards to Syria was heavily dependent on the provision of supplies provided by vassal rulers along the line of march. Inasmuch as military campaigning was confined to the time of the year known as the season in which 'the kings went forth to war', the long-term stocking up by vassals of provisions to feed the army would have required considerable notice. Reference to such advance warning is to be found in the El-Amarna letters where, for example, Arzawiya of Rukhizzi states '... The king my lord has written concerning preparations for the arrival of troops of the king my lord, and for the arrival of his many commissioners.'

Once away from the territories under firm Egyptian control the army would need to fall back upon stored provisions carried in wagons drawn by oxen. Those benefiting from these supplies would be the officers and senior ranks. No doubt other vehicles carried fodder for the vital chariot teams. Notwithstanding the undoubted efficiency of the scribes who oversaw the provision of supplies and rations, Bronze Age logistics were simply not up to the task of catering for the needs of all the troops in a corps on the march. For a force of 5,000 men the supply train would not only have been very large but also slow — oxen are not renowned for rapidity of movement! The more lowly soldiery were forced, as would many other armies throughout history, to live off the land. Indeed the exactitude with which scribes and quartermasters were trained to calculate supply needs and the reality of never having enough to feed all the soldiers in a corps is well addressed in a number of extant papyri.

By moving the army by corps and staggering their advance, a bivouacked force could support itself while not stripping the land for those following behind. In practice, positing a rate of advance of between 13 and 15 miles a day (this figure is not pulled out of the air, but is an average of those figures given for the advance of the Egyptian Army throughout the New Kingdom when moving from Egypt to Canaan and Syria, when such are mentioned) the distance between each army corps on a line of march towards a designated assembly point, in this case the Plain of Qadesh, would need to be about half that distance or less. Conveniently such a figure reveals itself in the text of the 'Poem' when the distance between Rameses, Amun and the corps of P'Re, crossing the ford 'south of the town of Shabtuna', is given as '1 iter' . The specificity with which this unit of distance is employed by the originator of the 'Poem' points very strongly to its being a standard measure drawn from a military manual or similar document. Highly variable figures have been proffered by commentators for this term, ranging from $1\frac{1}{2}$ miles to $12\frac{1}{2}$–$15\frac{1}{2}$ miles. Such variability is excessive. As the distance separating the corps of Amun and P'Re at the onset of the battle is itself of great significance in establishing a credible time-frame for the events that transpired, it is very important that we determine this distance with some degree of exactitude. In placing the camp of Rameses to the north-west of Qadesh, the distance to the ford would be about $7\frac{1}{2}$ miles with the notional value of '1 iter' corresponding to approximately $6\frac{1}{2}$ miles. Using this figure as a yardstick it could be shown how the second of two corps on a line of march, presuming a rate of advance suggested above, would always encamp in an area that had not been 'stripped bare' by foraging troops of the first corps. But the third and fourth corps, if advancing along the same axis, would never find very much in the way of sustenance.

Such eminently practical considerations have caused a number of commentators credibly to observe that the corps of Ptah and Sutekh may have followed a parallel line of march to Amun and P'Re along the west bank of the Orontes rather than follow directly in the footsteps of the two leading divisions as they advanced on the eastern side, as is nor-

mally assumed. Such may also be supported by a reference in the 'Poem' to Ptah 'being to the south of the town of Aronama' which is on the western bank of the river. Indeed it is because Ptah possibly had no need to ford the river at Shabtuna, as had Amun and P'Re, that it was able to advance relatively quickly to support Rameses, once word of his predicament had been received from the Pharaoh's Vizier, who had been dispatched specifically for that purpose before the battle. Nevertheless, most commentators have assumed that all four corps advanced along the eastern bank of the Orontes.

◀ *By the time of Qadesh in 1300 the Egyptian army was a highly professional force of elevated social standing within Egypt. Notwithstanding the introduction of the chariot arm at the beginning of the 18th Dynasty, it was still essentially an infantry army. The Rameside infantry shown here carry their shields strapped across their backs and in addition to their spears carry either a bronze-headed battleaxe or the sickle sword known as the 'khopesh'.*

▶ *19th Dynasty Nubian archer. Nubia was valuable to the New Kingdom pharaohs, not only for its supply of gold and other products and resources, but also for its manpower. Nubians served as mercenary infantry, putting to good use their noted skills with the bow. They retained their distinctive costume and served in their own units. Each of the four corps at Qadesh would have deployed Nubian archers. Angus McBride)*

The Combat Arms

Unlike the Hittites whom they were preparing to fight, the power of the Egyptian soldiery was vested in its infantry rather than chariot arm. It is in this way that the New Kingdom Egyptian army demonstrates a remarkable continuity with the military forces of the Old and Middle Kingdoms. This is not surprising because Egypt always possessed a larger native population than did her enemies and was therefore able to use it to provide the backbone of its military power. Although with the arrival of the chariot mobility was conferred and developed into a highly effective striking arm, even at the height of its military prestige the army was still built around the infantry companies of the respective army corps.

35

▲ One of the earliest extant depictions of a mounted horseman dating from the reign of Horemheb is to be seen in the bottom left-hand corner of this picture. The employment of the donkey seat shows that much expertise had still to be gained in the riding of horses. Of note also is the relatively small size of the animal which today would be likened more to a large pony.

▲ The basic inventory of weaponry used by the Egyptian infantryman at Qadesh. With the composite bow are the bronze-headed battleaxe, the khopesh sword and the bronze thrusting dagger.

The latter three weapons were used by the close-combat troops. The composite bow was very powerful and was the principal offensive weapon of both the infantry and the chariotry.

The use of large numbers of infantry also allowed the Egyptians to exploit the national experience in the mobilization and administration of large bodies of men for the great pharaonic building projects. Such expertise translated itself naturally to the army which adopted many of the administrative procedures employed for such purposes within Egypt.

Organization: The Infantry

The 4,000 infantry of an army corps were organized into twenty companies or 'sa' of between 200 and 250 men each. Their *esprit de corps* was fostered by the adoption of distinctive Standards many of whose names (from the New Kingdom) have survived.

Most predate the Rameside period as in the cases of 'Bull in Nubia', 'the Aten glitters', 'prowling lion', 'Menkepere: the destroyer of Syria', 'Manifest in Justice' and 'Splendour of Aten' from the reign of Amenophis III. It is likely that from the time of Rameses II company names would have been in the same vein with specific allusions to pharaoh's royal titles and the dynasty's veneration of the god Sutekh.

Within each company the soldiers were further broken down into units of 50 men. In battle the companies would be drawn up in a phalanx; experienced soldiers (menfyt) serving in the front ranks, recruits (nefru) and reserves to the rear. Foreign soldiers, of whom there were many in the Rameside army, maintained their own identity, either serving within the army corps or employed as additional units alongside the regular native Egyptian troops. Companies of Libyans, Nubians, Canaanite and Sherdens served with the Egyptians and although often described as 'mercenaries' were more likely impressed prisoners who preferred the life of a soldier in pharaoh's army to the alternative of slavery.

It is the 'nakhtu-aa' who are most frequently illustrated on Egyptian reliefs. These were the infantry known colloquially as the 'strong arm boys', specialists in close-quarters fighting and variously equipped with weaponry, shield and rudimentary body armour. The principal offensive weapon of the Rameside armies, however, was the composite bow. Employed in large numbers by the infantry and

chariot arms, and fired singly or in volleys, it was a deadly weapon in the hands of a trained archer.

The Chariotry

By the time of Qadesh the Egyptian chariot arm had a tradition of mobile warfare dating back nearly three hundred years. Large and magnificently

◀ *The war chariot of Rameses II. This plate illustrates very well the appearance of Pharaoh as he led the counter-attack against the Hittite chariotry during its assault on the encampment of Amun. Drawn by his two named horses, 'Victory-in-Thebes' and 'Mut-is-contented', and driven by his personal driver, Menna, Rameses prepares to fire his composite bow into the milling enemy chariotry. Shown to advantage is the bronze scale armour of the horses and the long scale coat of Pharaoh. (Angus McBride)*

equipped, the distinctive design of the Egyptian vehicle had reached the height of its development. Unlike its heavier Hittite contemporary the Egyptian chariot was designed above all for speed and manoeuvrability, its lightweight even delicate appearance disguising what was a very strong and robust vehicle. Herein lay the key to its battlefield deployment. Its offensive power lay not in its weight but in its capacity rapidly to turn, wheel and repeatedly charge, penetrating the enemy line and functioning as a mobile firing platform that afforded the 'seneny' or fighting crewman the opportunity to loose many arrows from his composite bow. The tactic was to avoid, if possible, becoming embroiled at close-quarters where the Hittite vehicles with their three-man crews and long spears could dictate the combat. It was without doubt the versatility of the chariotry that saved the day for Rameses at Qadesh.

Unlike their Hittite brethren the chariotry did not operate as a totally independent arm but were attached to the infantry corps. By the time of Qadesh chariots were attached to a corps on the basis of 25 vehicles per company. Not all of these were the heavier combat types, many lighter vehicles being retained for scouting and communications duties. For combat, however, there was a hierarchy of organization wherein the chariots were deployed in troops of ten, squadrons of fifty and the larger unit called a pedjet, commanded by an officer with the title of 'Commander of a chariotry host' and numbering about 250 chariots.

It is not possible to be precise about the size of the Egyptian chariot force at Qadesh though it could not have numbered less than 2,000 vehicles spread through the corps of Amun, P'Re, Ptah and Sutekh, assuming that approximately 500 machines were allocated to each corps. To this we may need to add those of the Ne'arin, for if they were not native Egyptian troops their number may not have been formed from chariots detached from the army corps. What is clear is that a considerable number of the Egyptian chariot force was still on the road to Qadesh when the battle took place and never saw combat at all. Their arrival after the battle was over provided Rameses with a fresh body of chariotry, perhaps large enough to have dissuaded the Hittites from further combat. Indeed, if neither Ptah nor Sutekh were ever engaged, those available to

▲▼ *By the time of the Battle of Qadesh the Egyptian war chariot and its crew had evolved into a sophisticated and highly refined war machine. In its combination of mobility and firepower it could be said to be the ultimate expression of chariot warfare in the Bronze Age. Originating in the Canaanite designs bequeathed by their Hyksos mentors, they had by the time of Qadesh become distinctively 'Egyptian'. Lightness of design was always a characteristic of the Egyptian chariot and this has frequently been equated with structural weakness. Such was far from the case, and in a real sense the features of the design represent the optimum compromise between lightness and strength. The photograph which illustrates a lightweight chariot from the reign of Amenophis III shows the features common to all Egyptian chariot types. In particular the axle at the rear of the cab, and the widely spaced wheels facilitated the remarkably small and fast turning-circle so vital to Egyptian tactics. The heavier war chariot shown below was structurally stronger in order to accommodate the range of weapons carried, and the scale armoured 'seneny' or archer who employed the composite bow in battle. Certainly was the highly effective use of the Egyptian chariotry at Qadesh that saved the day for Rameses.*

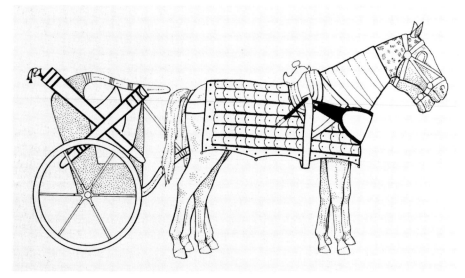

Pharaoh would have amounted to perhaps as many as half of those raised for the campaign. The great achievement of the Egyptians at Qadesh was to have so blunted the offensive might of the Hittite chariotry as to deprive Muwatallish of the very weapon upon which the Hittites depended for victory.

▶ *This wall painting, from the tomb of Kenamon at Thebes and dating from the reign of Amenophis II, illustrates the essential features of the bronze scale armour worn by many of the fighting crewmen at Qadesh. Other designs, including that worn by Pharaoh in the battle and shown elsewhere in this text ,suggest that smaller scales were used.*

▼ *While not historically accurate in every respect, the following stills from* the Cecil B. De Mille's 1956 version of **The Ten Commandments** *conveys in a highly effective manner the appearance of Rameside chariotry. Many of the essential features of the chariots used at Qadesh have been well reproduced. The most obvious anachronism is the use of metal and plastic rather than wood for the six-spoked wheels. Nevertheless, these reconstructions convey extremely well the apparent lightness of design of the Egyptian cab.(BFI)*

▲ *A superb shot illustrating Egyptian mass chariotry. What is well conveyed is the density of such vehicles on the move and the impression given of the length of line of what is actually quite a small number. Seen here is a squadron of fifty chariots. These would normally have been under the command of an officer known as the 'Standard-Bearer of Chariot Warriors'. In each of the Egyptian army corps there were 200-250 of these, or four or five squadrons. If one examines the photograph of the Arab wagon fording the Orontes 'south of Shabtuna', later in the text, it becomes clear that the passage of such numbers of chariots would have taken no small amount of time. How*

much credibility therefore can we ascribe to the Rameside claim that in the first wave of the Hittite attack 2,500 chariots forded the Orontes to assault the corps of P'Re and attack the camp of Amun. The crossing of such a huge number of chariots would have taken many hours. If the supposition is correct we are in fact positing a far smaller Hittite chariot force than has hitherto been assumed.(BFI)

◀ *In this shot from* **The Ten Commandments** *Rameses carries one of the long heavy arrows which are frequently seen transfixing the bodies of dead Hittites at Qadesh. Fired from the very powerful composite bow, they were designed to penetrate the bronze scale armour worn by many Hittite chariot crews. The upright lion motif on the bow case attached to the front right side of the cab was particularly venerated by Rameses II and was a symbol of power and the will to fight.*

▶ *The Sherden warriors that formed part of the élite guard of Rameses II at Qadesh are well attested to in a number of the reliefs depicting the battle. These foreigners had been brought into the army following their capture earlier in Pharaoh's reign when they had raided the Nile delta. Their fighting abilities and particularly their weaponry, in the form of their long swords, had made a great impression on the Egyptians. (Rob Chapman)*

THE BATTLE OF QADESH

So it was that Rameses II, King of Upper and Lower Egypt, awoke in his tent on the morning of Day 9, in the third month (late May) of the summer season in the fifth year of his reign. Encamped among the troops of the senior corps of Amun, the van of the Egyptian army lay approximately one day's march from Qadesh, in the 'hill country to the south' of the city. The site of Pharaoh's nocturnal abode was identified earlier this century by the American Egyptologist and archaeologist Henry Breasted: a very high and conspicuous mound, known as Kamuat el-Harmel, towering some 600 feet above the east bank of the River Orontes. To the rear of Pharaoh and separated from one another by approximately half a day's march lay the corps of P'Re, Ptah and Sutekh.

While this much is certain, what happens hereafter, based upon the less than specific and varying accounts in the Rameside inscriptions, behoves the reader to be conscious of the difficulties posed in reconstructing events with the seeming exactitude and certainty presumed elsewhere. Indeed, the manner in which the accounts in the 'Poem', 'Bulletin' and 'reliefs' appear to dovetail rather than agree, poses many problems and leaves many important questions about the battle unresolved. Not least of the observations is that the events which collectively form the 'battle' require a longer time-frame than is so often presumed in other accounts. In fact, apart from the one reference in the Poem that fixes Pharaoh's camp to the south of Qadesh on Day 9, there are no other attributions to specific dates. So time, as a dimension within the inscriptions, becomes telescoped and events when read in an uncritical fashion flow in one continuous narrative. This has frequently been reproduced in commentaries on the battle to give the impression that all that transpired in the way of battle occurred on Day 9. It is the view argued herein that such could not have been the case and that the main 'battle' took place on Day 10, that is the day after Rameses and the corps of Amun encamped on the Plain of Qadesh. Only a time-frame such as the latter takes account of the practical complexities attendant on operations of Late Bronze Age armies, which any credible narrative of the battle must do.

In accord with the plan of campaign agreed between Rameses and his generals, he and Amun struck camp shortly after daybreak on Day 9 with a view to reaching the designated camp site on the Plain of Qadesh before nightfall. There can be no suggestion that the army was advancing into 'territories new'. Qadesh and its environs was a 'stamping ground' of old acquaintance for the Egyptian army. Indeed, there must have been many soldiers and officers in the various corps who could remember vividly the great battle they fought beneath the walls of Qadesh with their young king's father. We have every reason for believing that Rameses shared this memory, having been present as crown prince. Drawing on this earlier experience, the location of the camp site was in all likelihood already determined. Despite the subsequent turn of events, we must suppose therefore that Rameses and his generals presumed that within a few days the four corps of the Egyptian army and the Ne'arin from the land of Amor would be concentrated on the Plain of Qadesh. This is a reasonable assumption because, as we shall see, although the arrival of the Ne'arin on Day 10 was indeed highly fortuitous given Pharaoh's desperate predicament, it was not at all unexpected. Had matters come to pass as Pharaoh originally intended, the concentration of the Egyptian army on Qadesh would have been effected by Day 11, but it would not have been ready to fight for some days thereafter — men and horses on either side needing time to recover from the strenuous exertions of a month on the march.

It is very important to reiterate that neither Rameses nor Muwatallish was in any doubt that

Qadesh was the venue for the battle. We have already noted that the time and place was in all probability determined in advance. Such was required by the very limited logistical capabilities of Bronze Age armies in the ancient Near East. There could be no notion of strategic surprise being realized through a wide-ranging war of manoeuvre. What constituted the equivalence in this campaign would be readiness for battle after arrival off the march. While the two kings knew the venue for battle and approximately when it was likely to take place, neither could know until contact was made by their respective armies where exactly the other was. More importantly, they were totally dependent on the eyes and ears of their scouts to deliver into their hands the vital piece of information that would give them the decisive advantage over the other once contact had been established. Was the enemy ready for battle? For if one was ready and the other not, it would be the former who would dictate the battle, maximizing to the utmost the particular skills, tactics and equipment of his own army. It is only when we appreciate how absolutely vital such an advantage would give the respective contenders can we begin to understand what now transpired.

Deception

Throughout the morning Rameses and the corps of Amun descended from the hill country and having emerged from the forest of Robawi began the slow and ponderous crossing of the Orontes in the vicinity of Shabtuna. Interestingly one of the more recent topographical surveys of the area has identified Shabtuna with Tell Ma'ayan which lies some 3½ miles to the north of the ford that was in all probability used by the Egyptians. Indeed nowhere in the inscriptions is the ford stated to be at Shabtuna itself, although this has been presumed and stated repeatedly by other commentators. The largest settlement close to the original crossing point is Ribla, whose own claim to fame would come from its employment as a base by Nebuchadnezzar II of Babylon when directing from afar, the siege of Jerusalem some seven centuries later.

As the advanced unit of the Egyptian army, Amun had a far larger baggage train than either of the other three corps. It is clear from the reliefs showing the camp established by Rameses at Qadesh that many of his personal household were in attendance. Not only were a number of the royal princes with their father but many servants and scribes of the royal household to attend the needs of their august and divine Lord. The 'tail' of the corps was therefore quite long and the fording of the Orontes in all likelihood took quite some time, from mid to late morning through to perhaps early afternoon. Perusal of the photograph of the Arab donkey team and cart fording the river in what is thought to be the general vicinity of the Egyptian crossing reveals

▶ *Fording the River Orontes today in the vicinity 'of the ford at Shabtuna'. It was in this area that Rameses and the corps of Amun crossed prior to advancing on Qadesh on Day 9, having descended from the hills to the south. Earlier comments about the rather careless manner in which 'fording' is explained away as if it were an activity of no moment is belied by this image. It would probably have taken Amun more than a few hours to have crossed the Orontes. (P. Parr)*

Hatti and its Syrian Vassals on the Eve of Qadesh *c.* 1300 BC

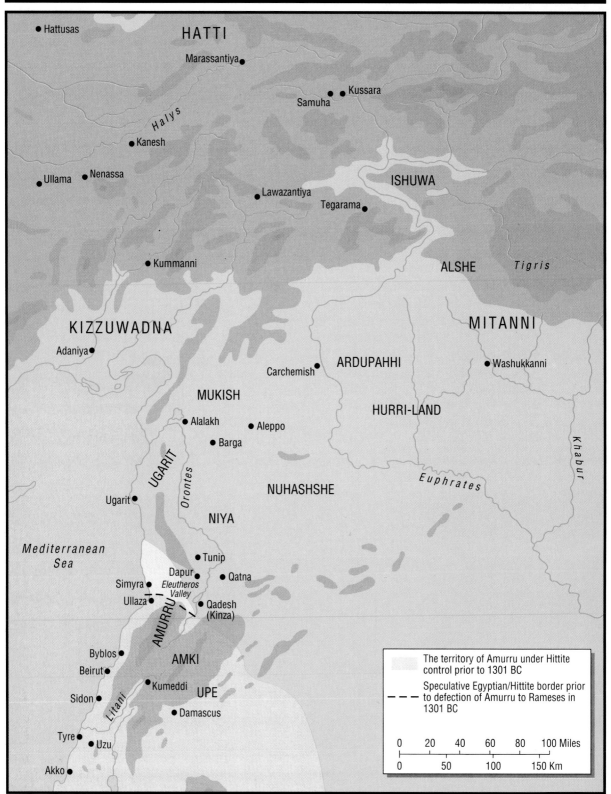

- Hattusas
- HATTI
- Marassantiya
- Kussara
- Samuha
- *Halys*
- Kanesh
- Ullama
- Nenassa
- ISHUWA
- Lawazantiya
- Tegarama
- Kummanni
- ALSHE
- *Tigris*
- KIZZUWADNA
- MITANNI
- Adaniya
- Carchemish
- ARDUPAHHI
- Washukkanni
- MUKISH
- HURRI-LAND
- Alalakh
- Aleppo
- Barga
- UGARIT
- *Orontes*
- *Khabur*
- *Euphrates*
- NUHASHSHE
- Ugarit
- NIYA
- *Mediterranean Sea*
- Tunip
- Dapur
- Qatna
- Simyra
- *Eleutheros Valley*
- Ullaza
- Qadesh (Kinza)
- AMURRU
- Byblos
- AMKI
- Beirut
- Kumeddi
- Sidon
- UPE
- *Litani*
- Damascus
- Tyre
- Uzu
- Akko

Legend:
- The territory of Amurru under Hittite control prior to 1301 BC
- – – – Speculative Egyptian/Hittite border prior to defection of Amurru to Rameses in 1301 BC

| 0 | 20 | 40 | 60 | 80 | 100 Miles |
| 0 | | 50 | 100 | | 150 Km |

◀ *The army raised by Muwatallish to contest possession of the city of Qadesh (Kinza) with Rameses II was in all probability the largest ever raised by the Hittite empire. Unlike that fielded by Egypt, it was very much an 'allied' army. Satellite kingdoms and vassal states all contributed to the force raised by the Hittite king to destroy the military ambitions of Egypt in central Syria and beyond.*

▶ *This map shows the major features of the city of Qadesh (Kinza) at the time of the battle in 1300. Rameses' camp on the night of Day 8/9 has been identified with the Kamuat El-Harmel('1'). The forest of Robawi, through which the corps of Amun passed on the morning of Day 9 was in the vicinity of ('2'). Passage of the Orontes was in all probability via the ford ('3') at Ribla, referred to in the inscriptions as being 'south of the town of Shabtuna'('4'). From there Amun made straightaway across the plain to establish the camp of Pharaoh ('1') to the north-west of Qadesh ('8'). The following day P'Re followed the same route and was in the general area of ('6') when the Hittite chariot force crossed the Al-Mukadiyah and assaulted them in the flank. At this time the bulk of the Hittite forces remained in the camp at Old Qadesh ('9'). The Wadi Halid ('1') marks the eastern entrance to the Eleutheros valley and it*

was from there that the Ne'arin made passage on to the northern Plain of Qadesh on the late morning of Day 10.

that the water reaches as high as mid wheel. The passage of three thousand years has not, it would seem, altered the rate of flow or direction of the Orontes here to any great degree. It does not take much imagination to see that the fording of this river by more than 500 chariots, 4,000 infantry, numerous donkey teams and carts pulled by oxen would have taken a very long time. The glib manner in which some commentators speak of the 'crossings of fords' by Egyptians and Hittites without considering the practical and time-consuming difficulties involved verges on the credulous. That the business was slow and laborious has very significant implica-

Qadesh and Environs

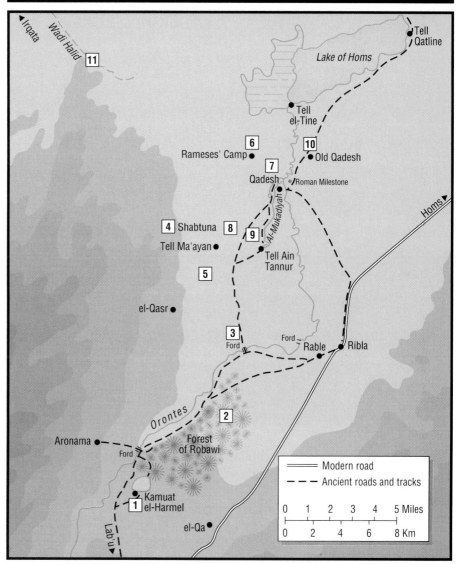

A

tions for understanding subsequent events.

It was shortly after the Orontes had been crossed that two Shasu bedouin were encountered and hauled before Pharaoh. There is no doubt in the Bulletin that the information they proffered to Rameses was false. Indeed, when questioned they reported that Muwatallish and the Hittite army was nowhere near Qadesh '...for the Fallen one of Hatti [Muwatallish] is in the land of Khaleb, to the north of Tunip'. If indeed they had been briefed by the Hittite monarch as to what to say to the young Pharaoh, clearly Muwatallish knew his man. In a deliberate ploy to massage the ego of the vain Egyptian king, the bedouin were told to say that it was because Muwatallish was afraid of Pharaoh that his army had not come to the city! The presumption that this was a ruse by the wily Hittite monarch, designed to lower Pharaoh's guard, has done much to establish his reputation as a clever strategist. There can be no doubting the Hittite king's motivation. In the words of the Bulletin the Shasu were dispatched specifically to '...prevent his majesty from making ready to fight with the Fallen one of Hatti'. An Egyptian army arriving on the Plain of Qadesh in piecemeal fashion, deluded into believing

▲ *This is the view of Qadesh that Rameses and the corps of Amun would have seen as they moved up from the south. Qadesh itself would have stood proudly against the skyline on the Bronze Age mound marked 'A'. The line of vegetation marks the Al-Mukadiyah tributary of the Orontes. It was across this and from the tree line that the Hittite chariots would have emerged to attack the corps of P'Re. Indeed, this picture gives an excellent view of the likely proximity of the Egyptian force relative to the Al-Mukadiyah when attacked. The short distance and suitability of the ground for chariot warfare shows how difficult it would have been for the rapidly advancing Egyptian column to have had time to effect any defensive deployment before the Hittite force hit the flank of the corps. (P. Parr)*

it had arrived first, would not only need time to recover and prepare for battle but would have been lulled into a false sense of security and therefore would have been psychologically unprepared for the storm about to break over them. With the Hittite multitude in place and rested, Muwatallish could deploy his army and force the battle long before Rameses was ready. In the race for strategic advantage on the Plain of Qadesh, Hatti had indeed won!

There was no attempt in Egyptian accounts to disguise the gullibility of Pharaoh in accepting this information at face value and in consequence embarking on a course of action that brought the Egyptian army to the verge of catastrophe. One can only surmise that his mind had become so addled by the vista of possibilities opened up by this purported news of Hatti's non arrival at Qadesh that his judgement became temporarily impaired. Perhaps his still limited experience as military leader compounded by a gratuitous self-confidence and strong personal sense of his own destiny allowed him to divine in this fortuitous turn of events the hand of 'his father', the god Amun. Eschewing the need for confirmation of the information from his scouts and riding roughshod over the views of his senior officers, he ordered the corps on to Qadesh forthwith.

The exact position of the Egyptian encampment has not been established, but it is very likely to have been in almost the same position as that used by Seti some years before. With access to a water supply it would have been an appropriate site for the Eqyptian army to camp and wait, so it was by now assumed, the army of Hatti. In a manner that prefig-

▲ *In this view of Tell Nebi-Mend from the south-east, the Bronze Age mound lies on the right of the tell. Hellenistic and Roman levels have been uncovered in the mid to lower (southern) parts of the tell. (P. Parr)*

ured the *castra* of the Roman legions of a millennium later, the troopers of Amun set out their camp. A defensive perimeter and embankment was dug and the shields of the infantry were placed around the top for added protection. Within the camp all was being set up for an extended stay. At the centre was placed a shrine to the god Amun and the great tent of the Pharaoh wherein he could be attended by his retinue. Certainly all was well, for, 'His Majesty took his seat on a throne of gold'. As depicted in the reliefs of the battle the camp has an almost domestic air about it. In the complacency of this balmy early May evening with Pharaoh probably in fine fettle, believing he had stolen a march on his opponent, news arrived that must have shaken Rameses, albeit only temporarily, to the very core.

One of Pharaoh's scouts had returned with two prisoners found lurking near the Egyptian encampment. Refusing to talk, they were subjected to a

▼ *The view of Qadesh/ Hittite Kinza, as seen from the north-east. The Hittite encampment lay in this direction but some miles further north at the site of Old Qadesh. The suggestion is that Hittite movement towards Qadesh would have been screened by the vegetation on the banks of the Orontes as much as by the mound of Qadesh itself. The corollary, however, must also be accepted. In the absence of scouts Muwatallish could not have known the exact time that Rameses arrived and encamped on Day 9 because the Egyptian army on the plain to the west was screened from the Hittites. This illustration is also significant in showing how in reality the movement of the large Hittite army* *from its base north-east of Qadesh to the south of the city would have been a long and complex operation. It is highly doubtful that Muwatallish would have done this on the morning of Day 10 without knowing the strength of Rameses' army. (P. Parr)*

▶ *In this view from the mound looking east it is easy to see how Qadesh dominated the surrounding plain. Clearly seen is the slow meandering flow of the Orontes in its old age. It was not the Orontes that Hittite chariots forded in order to attack the corps of P'Re but the smaller Al-Mukadiyah tributary that flows in a north-south direction to the west of the tell. (P. Parr)*

heavy beating before being dragged into the 'Presence'. The questions Pharaoh put to them strongly suggest that he had not at that time begun to suspect the danger they represented. Then his majesty said to them, 'What are you?' Who they were as persons did not interest him, but he wanted to know who had sent them. In admitting to 'belonging' to the King of Hatti, the enemy scouts proceeded to disabuse Rameses of the notion that the Hittite

army lay some days away to the north and that in reality, 'They are furnished with their infantry and their chariotry carrying their weapons of warfare, and they are more numerous than the sand of the river banks. See, they stand equipped and ready to fight behind Qadesh the Old'. Rameses sat incredulous and then aghast as the full implications of the information rapidly sank home. As matters stood there could be no avoiding the overwhelming proba-

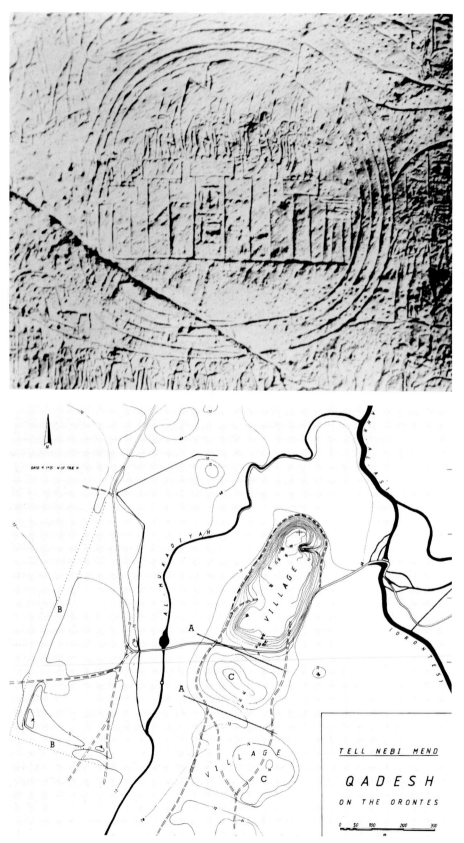

◀ Qadesh is depicted on reliefs at Luxor, at the Rameseum and at Abu Simbel (seen here). All three show variations in city details according to the particular artist, but the principal features and characteristics are clearly presented. Qadesh is shown as a well-fortified city built atop a high mound and surrounded by rivers and a moat (some say two moats). Two bridges spanning the moat gave access to and egress from the city.

◀ In this recent topographical survey of Tell Nebi-Mend there are a number of features of interest. The Bronze Age mound, on which the citadel of Qadesh, illustrated in the following photograph, was sited, lies to the north of the uppermost line marked 'A'. Both of those lines ('A') mark the possible site of the moat connecting the River Orontes on the left with Al-Mukadiyah on the right. A much later Roman or Byzantine ditch is shown by 'B' with 'C' denoting the position of the Hellenistic/Roman settlement on the tell. (P. Parr)

TELL NEBI MEND

QADESH

ON THE ORONTES

0   50   100   200   300
                m

bility that he and the Egyptian army stared absolute disaster in the face. Hastily convening a conference with his senior staff, Rameses revealed to them the dire predicament into which his earlier decision had led them. Concurrence was total that the only step to be taken was to effect a very rapid concentration of the three remaining corps on Qadesh. 'Then command was given to the Vizier to hurry on the army of His Majesty as they marched on the road to the south of the town of Shabtuna so as to bring them to where His Majesty was.' It also seems reasonable to suppose that a messenger was sent to expedite the arrival of the Ne'arin on the following day. To his chagrin Rameses realized that the Hittite monarch, who now 'stood ready to the north-east of the town of Qadesh', had clearly outfoxed him and that the initiative lay totally in the hands of Muwatallish.

What of the Hittites?

Any attempt to place the moves of Muwatallish and the Hittite host in some plausible sequence relative to Rameses' arrival at Qadesh must reject the account in the 'Bulletin' which has the Hittite army embarking on offensive action at the same time as Pharaoh is in conference with his officers. There are a number of reasons for this and they are worthy of exposition.

Not the least of them is the presumption that if the meeting of Rameses with his staff occurred in the evening of Day 9, as indeed was argued earlier, and we assume the account in the 'Bulletin' to be correct, we must posit a night attack by the Hittite king. While such a thing was not unknown at this time, the description in the 'Bulletin' that speaks of '.... the wretched Fallen one of Hatti was come with his infantry and his chariotry, as well as the many foreign countries that were with him' implies that the whole Hittite host was involved. In the light of the size of the Hittite force we can only surmise that such an operation, involving the crossing of the river in the growing darkness, would be a recipe for disaster. More importantly, the speed of the Hittite reaction to Pharaoh's arrival implied by the Bulletin means that the entire Hittite army was already standing to, and had been throughout the day, to the rear of Qadesh on the chance that Rameses would

arrive. Not only is the notion of 40,000 infantry and more than 3,500 chariots waiting patiently in the growing heat of the early Syrian summer with the wind blowing dust off the plain and into their faces a nonsense, it simply does not square at all with the observation that Muwatallish could only have known late on Day 9 that Rameses had in fact actually arrived. This would have been far too late in the day to begin deploying an army the size of that which the Hittites had encamped to the north-east of Qadesh.

Such Intelligence that he possessed had come to the Hittite king from two sources. The most important of these was in all probability the two Shashu bedouin who, having been released by the Egyptians, scuttled back to their master with the news that Rameses and the corps of Amun was in the 'neighbourhood south of Shabtuna'. The other came from the scouts whom Muwatallish had dispatched later that day to identify the specific location of Pharaoh's camp. It seems eminently reasonable to assume that other scouts apart from the two captured were involved in reconnoitring the locale of the Egyptians. Indeed, the lateness of the hour of those captured does suggest they were sent out following receipt of the Intelligence from the bedouin who had returned by late afternoon. We can surmise therefore that by the end of Day 9 the Hittite king knew the location of Pharaoh's camp, but did not know how many troops were there. The presumption must be that Muwatallish, in the knowledge that his army was fully rested and ready for combat, had determined to take action of some sort on the following day. What is now at issue is the nature of that action, because there are very good grounds for supposing that at this stage neither he nor Rameses was contemplating a full-scale battle on the morrow.

The Advance of P'Re

It was in the early hours of the morning of Day 10 when the Vizier approached the camp of the corps of P'Re which, if earlier reasoning is sound, lay bivouacked in the vicinity of the ford at Ribla. In the cold, early morning light the troops were still sleeping after the exertions of the previous day's march. Excepting the few teams on guard duty, the chariots were all unhitched and the horses tethered. The

tranquillity of the dawn scene was broken by the unexpected arrival of the chariot bearing Pharaoh's chief minister. There followed a flurry of activity as senior officers of the corps were awakened to hear the urgent summons of their Lord. In an obvious state of agitation the Vizier commanded them in the name of Rameses to march forthwith on Qadesh. Across the camp a succession of orders were barked out, signal trumpets sounded and drums were beaten. Men still heavy from sleep were shaken or kicked into consciousness and ordered to make ready for a rapid departure. Notwithstanding the urgency that now attended their exertions, it must have taken the corps more than a few hours to prepare to march as tents were taken down, horses fed and the ass teams and ox-wagons loaded. The Vizier, having received a fresh team of horses, had

already driven off southward to rouse the corps of Ptah which lay 'south of the town of Aronama' (the commentary linked to the reliefs at Abu Simbel has Pharaoh's butler and a mounted messenger attending to the same task. It is not unreasonable to suppose that they were dispatched at different times on the following day).

More hours were expended as P'Re forded the Orontes, negotiating with some difficulty the banks churned-up by the corps of Amun the previous day. It is entirely conceivable that in the urgency to reinforce Pharaoh the cohesion of the corps began to break up once the western bank was reached. In their desire to assist their Lord a certain degree of military caution may well have been set aside, and some of the chariot units may have been sent on ahead. If, strange as it might seem, the troops of

◄ *The line of vegetation that lies across the picture marks the Al-Mukadiyah tributary of the Orontes. Beyond is the plain on which the battle took place, extending 3-4 miles to the foothills of the Lebanese mountains. In antiquity the plain would not have been cultivated so it would have been a perfect arena for the manoeuvre of masses of chariotry, providing optimum physical conditions for their employment. The Hittite attack on P'Re, which would have been marching from left to right at some indeterminate distance from the Al-Mukadiyah, would have emerged from the line of vegetation having forded the tributary. It is easy to see how, having been scattered by the assault on their flank, there was very little cover for the panicking Egyptian soldiers, many of whom would have been ridden down by the Hittites. (P. Parr)*

Qadesh was perceived by both sides in terms of early arrival at the designated battleground. The longer an army was rested prior to battle, the greater its advantage in determining the outcome. Furthermore, respect for legal propriety and protocol were characteristic of Hittite relations with vassal states and other powers. It is surprising therefore that Muwatallish is held in high esteem for initiating battle without observing the very protocol he may well have taken great care to uphold. Now this may or may not have been the case at Qadesh, but there are more than a few pointers to suggest that what has become known as 'The Battle of Qadesh' may not have been the contest that either Rameses or his Hittite opponent desired or intended. Paradoxically, what has come to be regarded as the archetypal battle initiated by guile and ruse may in reality have been anything but!

Combat is Joined

The sun was already climbing above the early morning mist when the corps of P'Re, having forded the cold waters of the Orontes, began final assembly prior to moving off in the direction of Pharaoh's camp which lay some 6½ miles to the north.

Word had already passed along the column from the 'mer-mesha' that the march northwards would be at a rapid pace, urgency was the order of the moment! For the 'menfyt' in the front ranks of the infantry column, grizzled veterans of both Seti and Rameses' earlier campaigns, the experience of the battle march was hardly novel. For those whose first campaign this was, however, the urgency of the past few hours would have found them nervous and in a state of anxiety, unsure of what was to come. Over the past month many of the veterans would, after their own fashion, have encouraged the 'nefru' now assembled in the rear of the column. Notwithstanding the hard training these youngsters had received in the 'sekheperu' under the ever watchful eye of their harsh drill sergeants, it is clear that the long march from Egypt and through Canaan had exhausted many of them. For some, the care extended to these novice soldiers derived from a genuine paternalism, more than a few of the veterans having sons in the ranks with them for the first time. Such was the visible expression of the generational com-

P'Re were unaware that fighting was imminent, that too would begin to explain what now came to pass.

In a real sense our ability to understand the 'battle' that now took place turns heavily on whether action was deliberately initiated by the Hittites or whether what transpired was a mistake. Speculation of this sort arises from a consideration of the part that protocol played in determining the procedures for giving battle in antiquity, and the extent to which the Egyptians and Hittites at Qadesh were governed by these. Armies would first encamp and combat would be joined by agreement, not initiated by surprise attack. Indeed, there is evidence to suggest that in the Ancient Near East the employment of surprise as a means of securing strategic military advantage was not regarded as legitimate. It has already been stressed that strategic surprise at

pact between Pharaoh and his army that allowed many of these men their own land in Egypt as long as a son was available when the time came to serve their Lord in the ranks. Now the day had come to repay their debt to Pharaoh on the field of battle.

Drifting along the column came the sound of the battle trumpets, their single discordant notes merging in a cacophony of noise signalling the beginning of the march. With a final barked order from the 'tjai-seryt', shields were slung across backs and spears and bows shouldered as one after another, with Standards raised high and to the fore, each 'sa' of infantry moved off. Soon a fast pace was being set. Little could be seen to the left or right of the column, the tramping feet and the chariots alongside raising clouds of fine dust to obscure all but the scene immediately ahead. Over the din came the faint sound of the battle songs of the 'menfyt' in the van, while from the rear came the refrain of stranger tongues signifying that the Nubian or Libyan auxiliaries were adding their offerings. But with the onset of the morning heat, the dull pain of aching limbs and the all-enveloping dust, the singing tailed off and all became quiet save for the raucous coughing of soldiers and the vibrating, rhythmic pummelling of thousands of marching feet. As Shabtuna fell away on the left of the column the view to the north-east became increasingly dominated by the tell of Qadesh, its great fortress standing proud against the deepening blue of the skyline and governing the surrounding plain. Above the crenellated battlements a large, striped Standard shaped like a sail flew in the breeze. To the right of the column and just over three-quarters of a mile away, a vivid ribbon of green vegetation marked the beginnings of Al-Mukadiyah, the tributary of the Orontes which flowed alongside the base of the tell and then to the south of the city. Here the scrub of the plain's edge gave way to a more luxuriant growth of bushes, shrubs and trees that obscured the flatness beyond. It was from this treeline, which offered such superb cover, that a mass of Hittite chariotry now sortied, hurtling upon the Egyptian corps. The Egyptian chariotry screening the right flank of the column had no time to react, being ridden down and submerged by a tidal wave of vehicles. Hardly had the heavier Hittite chariots begun to accelerate on the level of the plain than they were crashing into the

massed ranks of the Egyptian troops in the centre of the column, their momentum temporarily dissipated. The right flank of the column of P'Re collapsed as men were ridden down and crushed beneath the wheels and hooves of the Hittite chariots. Long spears flashed out to the left and right in an orgy of killing as Hittite warriors thrust at the falling infantry, the chariot drivers whipping their horses to a lather as they ploughed further into the rapidly disintegrating Egyptian ranks. Such was the crush and fear engendered by this ferocious assault that discipline evaporated, little or no resistance being put up by the infantry. Men cast aside shields, bows and other weapons. All was now panic as the cohesion of the corps vanished. In minutes, all order had gone in the face of this totally unexpected and unforeseen assault. More and more Hittite chariots rushed out on to the plain, emerging from a gap in the trees that marked the passage from the ford which minutes before they had crossed. Such was the confusion caused by so many chariots concentrated in such a short space that more than a few of the Anatolian machines overturned, flinging their crews beneath the hooves and wheels of the chariots behind. As the panic rippled through the Egyptian column the men at the front turned to witness the desperate predicament of their comrades. A broad swathe had been bloodily hacked through the centre of P'Re through which Hittite chariots were streaming and accelerating across the plain beyond. Unlike the lighter Egyptian machines, these heavier Hittite chariots were unable to execute rapid turns or changes of course without overturning. Moving westwards they were able to employ the space of the plain to begin a loping turn towards the north.

All happened so quickly that it took the senior officers at the front of the column some moments to establish what exactly was going on. Manoeuvring their chariots to gain a clearer view, they saw the corps disintegrating before their eyes; a wild mêlée of rushing chariots and fearful troops dispersing to all points of the compass. It was clear, however, that it was the long line of Hittite chariots purposefully heading on to a parallel track to the west of the column, and seemingly oblivious of the Egyptian chaos around them, that now posed the greatest threat. There could be no doubting the Hittite intention. Little could be done now to save P'Re, so without

▶ *This variation in detail is noticeable in the depiction of Qadesh at the Rameseum. The rendition is less well executed than that at Abu Simbel or at Luxor, but what remains apparent, however, is the very strong position of the site.*

further ado the Egyptian chariot squadrons milling around at the head of the column were dispatched north to warn Pharaoh of the imminence of the Hittite attack. With a crack of their whips the kedjen of each chariot accelerated his team as rapidly as possible, mindful of the Hittite column by now on the far side of the plain and on a matching course, trailing a huge, rising plume of dust as they too accelerated towards the camp of Amun and Rameses.

The Hittite Assault

Throughout the early morning the sentries on the shield wall in the camp of Amun had been under orders to keep a sharp watch for evidence of the advance of P'Re. The monotonous flatness of the plain to the south made it difficult to see clearly the onset of a large column of troops at a distance. This was compounded by the heat haze which by mid morning was causing the air to shimmer, and the fine dust whipped up by the wind from the surface did much to diffract the clear light of this early Syrian summer day. Although the camp had been tense throughout the night following the alarming news of the proximity of the Hittite army on the far bank of the Orontes, there was little suggestion that Amun was in danger of attack. Combat it was assumed was still some days away, although there were few within

the shield wall who were so complacent that they did not wish for the rapid arrival of the rest of the army. As the process of pitching the camp had not yet been completed it had been thought prudent to keep at least some of the troops standing to arms and a number of infantry companies and chariot squadrons were held ready for action. If all went well the corps of P'Re and Ptah, having been summoned in some urgency by Pharaoh's Vizier, would arrive by nightfall with Sutekh following early the next day. On the north wall other eyes were turned to the mountains from where it was assumed the Ne'arin would arrive shortly, having marched through Amurru via the Eleutheros valley.

It was the urgent and insistent shouts from the guards on the southern shield wall that gave the first intimation that things were wrong. Jabbing fingers on outstretched arms directed the attention of the officers to the dust clouds coming up from the south. While the cloud to the left was clearly approaching the camp more quickly, that to the right was growing visibly larger with every passing moment. Experienced eyes quickly recognized the telltale signs of chariots at speed and the shout went out across the camp announcing the imminence of their arrival, although uncertain as to their origin. It was only by a margin of a few minutes that the first of the surviving chariots of P'Re raced into the

1 *Having been awakened in the early hours of the morning by the vizier of Rameses II with an urgent summons to come to Pharaoh's aid, the corps of P'Re crosses the Orontes at the ford in the vicinity of Ribla and begins a rapid march across the plain towards the camp of Amun, which lies just over 1 iter (approx. 7 miles) to the north.*

Shabtuna

EG
XXXX
RAMESES II

2 *The Hittite king, hearing of the arrival of Rameses the previous evening, orders a detailed reconn-aissance in force of the Egyptian camp the following morning. A large chariot detachment moves south-wards from the camp, then skirts the tell on which Qadesh is sited, and crosses the Orontes.*

3 *It is now probably mid-morning and, having traversed the cultivated fields to the south of the tell, the Hittite chariot column crosses the Al-Mukadiyah tributary and emerges from the tree-line that has thus far been shielding its movements. It finds itself confronted by the north-wards-moving column of P'Re less than a mile away.*

4 *With momentum building up in the column, and with no space in which to manoeuvre their chariots, the Hittites have no recourse but to 'crash into' the*

Hittite chariots

Plain of Qadesh

Corps of P'Re

River Orontes

Egyptian corps and hack their way through. The Egyptian screening chariots on the right of the column are swept away by the onrush of the completely unexpected assault. Within moments the Egyptian column begins to disintegrate.

5 *At the head of the Egyptian column a bloody swathe is being cut through the centre of P'Re's corps as*

To Amurra

Camp of
Rameses II
and Amun

*the line of Hittite chariots
still emerging on to the plain
from the tree-line hacks its
way through to the far side.
A number of Egyptian
chariots are dispatched
northwards to warn
Pharaoh of the Hittite
attack.*

6 *Seemingly uninterested in
bringing about the
destruction of P'Re, the
Hittite chariot column uses
the width of the plain of
Qadesh to begin a turn to the
north in order to carry out
their primary orders of
reconnoitring the Egyptian
camp.*

Lake of Homs

2

Hittite
encampment at
'Old Qadesh'

HT | xxxx
MUWATALLISH

*Possible vantage point of
Hittite King Muwatallish*

Qadesh

Hittite reconnaissance
force

Al-Mukadiyah

7 *In the Egyptian camp,
only a few troops are to arms
when the chariots of P'Re
arrive with news of the
attack and the dust from the
Hittite column is made out
moving rapidly northwards.*
8 *The disintegration of the
corps of P'Re seems total,
with the surviving troops*

*dispersing to all points of the
compass. Nevertheless, the
bulk of them survive, and
many make their way to
Pharaoh's camp by
nightfall.*
9 *The Hittite column
crashes into the western side
of the camp of Amun.*

THE BATTLE OF QADESH

Phase One: The Hittite initial attack on the corps of P'Re and on the Egyptian camp

camp, the 'senenys' within pointing to the huge dust plume that was even then resolving itself into a mass of Hittite chariotry sweeping in from the west. The wave of panic that swept through Amun's camp was almost tangible. In a mad scramble infantry grabbed weapons that lay to hand and at the far end of the camp there was frantic urgency among the crews as they hitched up their teams to the chariot cabs. The Hittites, now clearly apparent in a huge and seemingly endless column, swept around the western and extreme northern end of the camp before crashing through the shield wall to begin their assault.

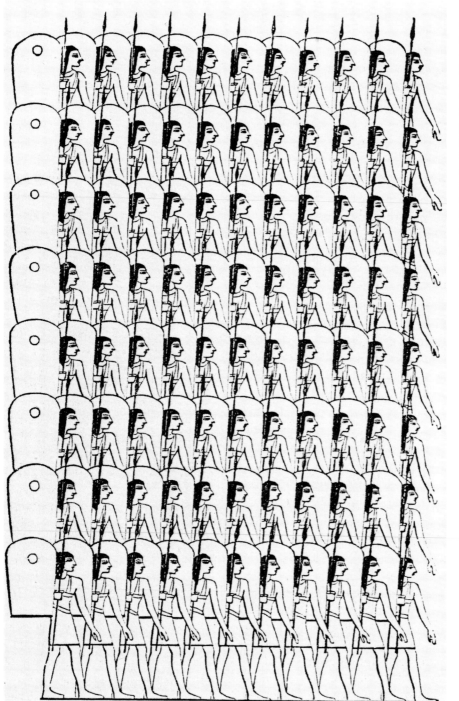

◀ New Kingdom infantry on the march are seen clearly in this reproduction based upon wall paintings from Theban tombs. The close order marching, with shields slung across the back, gives a good impression of the appearance of the infantry of P'Re when the Hittite chariot attack was launched. It is easy to see how a very sudden high-speed assault could have led to panic and the subsequent disintegration of the entire corps.

As the Anatolian warriors washed over the mass of Egyptian troops at the western end of the camp their surge was already beginning to dissipate. Chariots slowed as the numerous tents, stores and other impedimenta became as rocks breaking the tide. Amid the chaos of panicking Egyptian soldiers, those who had been standing to arms throughout the night sensed the slowing of the Hittite drive and advanced with khopesh or spear in hand to attack the enemy. A desperate hand-to-hand mêlée ensued as the Egyptians pulled down Hittite crews from their cabs or were transfixed by the long thrusting spears of the enemy. Chariots slowed to a crawl as horses struggled vainly to move forward, hemmed in by their own kind as more and more chariots crowded into the camp. Screams of the dying merged with the whinnying of terrified horses as they were killed by Egyptian archers firing into the mass of chariot teams. As they ground to a halt or collapsed, the crews were set upon by the Egyptians. More than a few of the survivors recalled the grotesque sight of Hittite crewmen hauled backwards by their long hair and dispatched by the flashing downward stroke of the 'menfyt' khopesh. More and more Hittite chariots ploughed into the camp and it was becoming apparent that many of the crews were less concerned with fighting Egyptians than in laying hands on the immense booty.

No sooner had the assault on the camp begun than Pharaoh's bodyguard had deployed to bar access to the royal enclosure. Veteran close-combat infantry squared off with the Sherden warriors who, in their horned helmets and with long swords in hand, prepared to receive the Hittite chariotry. Within all was haste. Pharaoh was hurriedly informed of what had transpired. Recovering rapidly from the surprise of the news of P'Re and the Hittite attack on the camp, he quickly, '... assumed the accoutrements of battle and girded himself with his corselet' and prepared to give battle with his household chariotry and the few squadrons readied for action at the rear of the camp, as yet untouched by the Hittite assault. Household staff rushed through the royal enclosure with Pharaoh's fan-bearer ushering the royal children, including Pharaoh's eldest son Prahiwenamef, to the safety of the opposite end of the encampment where they were placed under guard. His instructions to them were precise: 'Do not go out on the

west side of the camp and keep clear of the battle.' Donning the blue khepresh crown, Pharaoh mounted his chariot and with a terse command to Menna, his kedjen, led the available chariotry of the corps out of the eastern entrance of the camp at a fast gallop to begin deployment for a rapid counter-attack on the Hittite host.

The Egyptian column swept around towards the north-west and rapidly deployed into line of battle. As yet no Egyptian chariotry had taken on the Hittite attackers whose attention was now almost totally focused on the camp. Many were driving hither and thither, running down Egyptian infantry as they emerged from the camp in the hope of fleeing north. Amid the chaos, however, it was clear that the Hittites' cohesion was already lost, and in the milling of their numbers lay the opportunity for Rameses to effect some recovery of the dire Egyptian position. A rapid, albeit desperate and unsuspected counter-attack, exploiting the apparent fatigue of the Hittite chariot teams, their lack of cohesion, the dust cloud wafting across the field and above all the power and range of the Egyptian composite bows, was now launched. Under these conditions the much greater size of the Hittite force counted for little.

At a signal from Rameses the chariots began to roll and gather speed as they headed towards the milling mass of the enemy who appeared as yet to be unaware of their presence. Exploiting the range of their bows, the now rapidly moving Egyptians loosed their arrows and in a process reminiscent of their training procedures fired volley after volley into the densely packed and slowly moving Hittite chariot body. Approaching at speed, the Egyptians were able to effect a number of battle turns without making contact before the Hittites, reacting slowly to the sight of their compatriots falling around them and transfixed by arrows, realized they were under attack. The disciplined fire of the Egyptian senenys began to execute a fearful destruction. It was unnecessary for them to target an individual team for the concentration of the milling Hittite chariotry allowed each arrow in a volley to find a target. Ponderously the Hittites began to react to the counter-attack. More than a few, whipping their now tired teams, tried to close the distance with the Egyptians but were shot down as they approached. The surviv-

◄ *Rameses II, courtesy of Yul Brynner! This picture has been used to allow a closer view of the weaponry carried by a Rameside chariot at Qadesh and in particular that of the Pharaoh himself. The reproduction chariot was based on that showing Rameses in the Rameseum reliefs and is reproduced elsewhere in this book. Clearly seen is the composite bow in its case attached to the side of the cab, the long heavy arrows and the javelins used when forced into close combat or employed after the arrows had been exhausted.(BFI)*

▶ *Based upon a relief of Rameses found on the second pylon of the north tower on the western wall of the Rameseum. The small bronze scale armour corselet is clearly rendered and such is also seen employed on the horses. The Hittites are also depicted wearing scale armour. On the original painting they are coloured red and blue signifying either that they were actu-*

ing mass, however, already sensing that the initiative was slipping away attempted to disengage from the combat in the camp and effect a withdrawal to the south. They began to stream away in a disorganized rabble, heading back across the plain as fast as their rapidly tiring teams could pull them. In their rear Rameses, perceiving the shift of the flow of combat in his favour, ordered forward the still fresh Egyptian chariotry. A great cry went up from the troops in the camp, who only minutes before had been fighting for their very survival. Scampering over the mass of debris and ruined chariots, dead and dying men and horses that now littered the western end of the camp, they followed in the wake of the chariots racing past them, impromptu chariot runners deter-

mined to wreak vengeance upon their foes.

With Rameses in the van the Egyptian chariots swept around the western end of their devastated camp in pursuit of the retreating Hittites. More accurate archery was needed as the Hittite vehicles dispersed into individual targets. As the Egyptians closed the distance the fearful Hittite drivers whipped heir teams to a lather. The horses, however, now exhausted by the prolonged combat, slowed appreciably as they raced across the plain, seeking the security of the river. Without hesitation the Egyptian archers transfixed them and their crews with arrows and javelins. The retreat was rapidly becoming a rout as the passage of the Hittite force became littered by crashed and broken chariots. For

ally painted or simply rows of scales alternating with stitching. The length of the heavy arrows is apparent. Significantly horses are as frequent a target as the Hittite warriors who lie on the ground.

▶ A photograph of the image on the reliefs upon which the previous picture was based. The triumphant pose of Pharaoh in his chariot firing his composite bow and his horses trampling his enemies underfoot was a common artistic convention of the time.

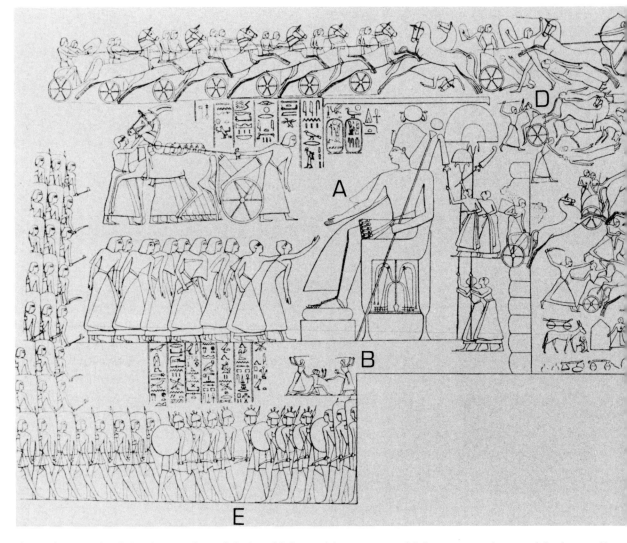

those that survived the destruction of their vehicles but lay pinned down or badly injured on the ground death came quickly. Egyptian foot soldiers following in the wake of the chariots dispatched them and hacked off a hand as a grisly trophy to prove their bravery so that after the battle the scribes could note their names as they contended for Pharaoh's attention and the 'gold of valour'.

Excursus One

What has been presented thus far is an attempt to render a coherent and realistic scenario of the somewhat terse accounts of the opening phases of the Hittite attack on P'Re and the assault on the camp of Amun given in the Poem and the Bulletin. A number of important points have been implied in

this account which are at variance with the traditional interpretation of the texts and the manner in which they have been represented in other commentaries and descriptions of the battle.

The first and most significant of these concerns the reaction of P'Re to the Hittite attack. That the corps disintegrated is accepted as being the likely outcome of its having been surprised on the march. But the unquestioned presumption, accepted by Rameses (although he may have had other motives for propagating this explanation of events) that P'Re panicked because they were skittish and cowardly seems at best dubious. It is more credible that such panic as did ensue was caused by the surprise and ferocity of the Hittite attack under conditions in which the Egyptians were totally unprepared and unable to respond. This was in all probability com-

▲ The image employed here is based upon one of a number of reliefs at Luxor depicting the Battle of Qadesh. Several observations need to be made concerning Egyptian artistic conventions prior to explaining its content. The first concerns the size of figure: the larger it is the more important the person. Thus Rameses dominates the scene. In addition the relief depicts in one image many events that were separated in time, so it is important to bear in mind the time-frame suggested in the text and place the events depicted in the relief in that context. In ('A') Pharaoh sits on his 'golden throne' with his back to the camp. He is approached by a group of senior officers who break the news to him that the Hittite king and his army, far from being 'to the north of Tunip' are already encamped in the vicinity of Qadesh. Above the officer group Pharaoh's chariot and his horses 'Victory-in-Thebes' and 'Mut -is-contented' are readied for battle by his driver and shield-bearer Menna. In the register below this scene ('B') is shown the beating of the Hit-

tite scouts caught late in the evening of Day 9. The text associated with the scene reads, 'The coming of Pharaoh's scout bringing two scouts of the Fallen one of Hatti into the Pharaoh's Presence. They beat them to make them say where the wretched Fallen one of Hatti was.' ('C') gives a remarkable insight into the earliest known depiction of a military camp which is enclosed by the shield wall ('F'). Apart from the royal enclosure there are unhitched chariots and horses, donkeys and other beasts of burden and the supplies they have brought. This calm atmosphere changes as the Hittite chariots reach the camp and begin to assault it ('D'), tempted by the booty within. To the left of the royal enclosure Egyptian soldiers can be seen dragging Hittite crews from their chariots and dispatching them with their khopesh swords and bronze daggers. There are a number of Egyptian chariots in action which belies the claim of Rameses that 'he stood alone' before the Hittite chariotry. 'E' illustrates Pharaoh's Sherden bodyguard with their characteristic horned helmets.

pounded by an expectation as they marched single-mindedly to join Amun that combat was not imminent! We are talking about one of the senior corps of the professional Egyptian army with a long and distinguished history and with much experience of fighting the Hittites. The notion that what transpired arose from their collective cowardice is not a credible explanation for their dissolution as a coherent fighting unit. Indeed, the Poem implies that many troops of P'Re were able to reach Pharaoh's camp with news of the attack. This does not suggest that everyone in the corps had lost his head!

What is most intriguing about the Hittite attack is that P'Re was not totally destroyed. By nightfall many of the troops had recovered to Pharaoh's camp. Wherein therefore lies the purported prescience attributable to Muwatallish in stationing his chariots in just the position to assault P'Re as it marched across the plain if the intention were not to destroy it? If Muwatallish desired the defeat of Rameses, destruction of Pharaoh's army rather than its scattering must have been his prime intention. Only by this means would he have been able to inflict upon Rameses the decisive outcome his strategy required. Why then, having found P'Re isolated and unprepared, did he not destroy the corps? It is really too disingenuous to argue that the Hittite chariotry had orders only to scatter the troops of Rameses. Indeed, it is a palpable nonsense to believe that the Hittite chariotry could only manage to achieve such a limited and contrived objective! Further grist to the mill derives from the failure of Muwatallish to deploy his infantry to effect the destruction of the Egyptian corps. Chariotry alone could not have defeated P'Re. Infantry would have been needed to follow-up the initial success of the purported surprise assault. In fact Hittite battlefield tactics presumed as much. The claim that he deliberately chose to employ his chariotry and consciously eschewed the use of his infantry is not tenable. Given the close proximity of the ford to the Egyptian column, the Hittite infantry would have needed to advance only a very short distance to close with the enemy. That they did not do so is highly significant. Such a major omission on the part of Muwatallish is very difficult to explain away and is inconsistent with the cunning and skill he is purported to have displayed in the battle. Such reason-

ing, however, takes at face value the Egyptian claim that the Hittite infantry were actually deployed for battle at Qadesh. There are strong grounds for believing that this was not the case. If the purpose of the surprise attack on P'Re were to maximize the military advantage to the Hittites of attacking isolated elements of the Egyptian army on the march, it must be argued that far from being the remarkable coup it has always been assumed, the Hittite attack was in reality a failure!

It is the contention of the author that the Hittite attack on the column was conducted on a very narrow frontage and that they were more concerned with cutting through the corps of P'Re than seeking its destruction. Why should this be? Quite simply, far from seeking to attack P'Re, the Hittite force did not know of its presence on the Plain of Qadesh prior to crossing the ford, and that its designated task was actually to undertake a reconnaissance in force of Pharaoh's camp. Muwatallish, aware of Pharaoh's presence, lacked as yet the Intelligence detailing the size of the Egyptian force. On possession of that information turned his willingness to deploy his forces for battle. Until such time as the first Hittite chariots emerged from the tree line and saw the corps of P'Re marching directly across their line of advance, they had no idea that the Egyptians were actually there. Given the size of the corps and its tail of ox-wagons, ass trains and so on, the column would have been about two miles in length and its line of march parallel to and not less than half a mile from the Mukadiyah tributary of the Orontes. This was a very short distance for a chariot to traverse. The time lapse between leaving the treeline of the Mukadiyah and crossing the half-mile of ground before hitting the right flank of P'Re would have been at the most a few minutes. This would not have given the Hittites or the Egyptians time to

▶ Egyptian 19th Dynasty chariot. In essence there was little difference between this Egyptian chariot and that ridden by Rameses II shown on page 63. The perspective does allow a good view of the wide wheel-base and the rear-mounted axle that endowed the Egyp- *tian vehicle with a superior manoeuvrability to that of its Hittite equivalent. The task of the runner would have been to follow as quickly as possible after the chariot and dispatch or capture Hittites wounded or rendered* **hors de combat** *in the charge.(Angus McBride)*

react. Certainly there was no space at all for the Hittites to manoeuvre in order to avoid the Egyptian column. With the Hittite force building-up to their rear as more chariots crossed the ford, the lead vehicles would have had no alternative but to drive into the Egyptian ranks and hack their way through!

Such would seem to be implied by Gardiner in his translation of the Qadesh inscriptions when he renders the account of the attack in the Poem as, '... now they came forth from the south side of Qadesh and broke into [?] the army of P'Re in its midst as they were marching and did not know nor were they prepared to fight'. 'Broke into' would seem to be the most apposite term in this context to describe the

▼ *The second of the graphic images based on the wall reliefs from Luxor concern the course of the fighting following the surprise Hittite attack on the camp of Amun. In ('A') Rameses, shown far larger than any other person on the battlefield, is depicted charging single-handed into the mass of Hittite chariotry. In the Abu Simbel reliefs a mounted rider is shown hurrying on the corps of Ptah whereas in the Luxor reliefs a chariot is hurriedly sent to summon them to the battlefield; whereas in ('C') Ptah arrives at the battlefield at a time at variance with the events shown in ('A'). If the reasoning offered in the text is valid Ptah would have had to make a very rapid forced march throughout the course of Day 10, arriving at Qadesh probably*

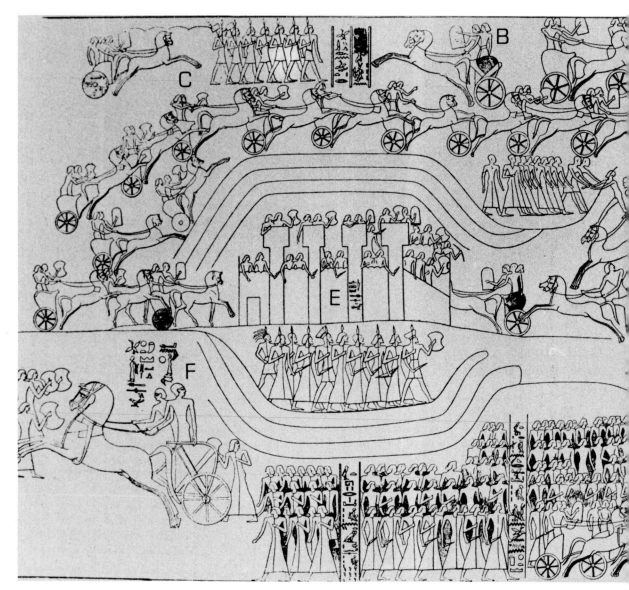

Hittite tactic! It is a *post factum* rationalization by both ancient and modern commentators that has ascribed to Muwatallish this foresight in launching his assault on the corps of P'Re. His reputation has benefited greatly from what was in all likelihood a remarkably fortuitous coincidence. In reality the Hittite chariot crews were as surprised to see the Egyptian column as their enemies were to be assaulted by them. The most telling testimony to this hypothesis is the track of the Hittite chariots north to Pharaoh's camp leaving behind the wreck of a shattered, but not destroyed Egyptian corps.

To propose the view that the Hittite chariot column was not engaged in a planned assault on P'Re

by mid afternoon. It is noticeable how Ptah's role in the battle is underplayed in the 'Poem' and the 'Bulletin'. The timely arrival of the Ne'arin ('D') earlier in the day undoubtedly saved Rameses from destruction. In ('E') retreating Hittite chariots are shown entering Qadesh itself, leaving in their wake a field strewn with their dead. One of the stranger aspects of

the Hittite strategy (if we assume the Egyptian accounts to be accurate) was the failure of Muwatallish ('F') to commit his infantry to support the chariot attack. They supposedly watched the Egyptian counter-attack from the opposite bank of the Orontes.

1 *Attracted by the prospect of booty, the Hittite chariot force crowds in on the western end of the Egyptian camp. Some of the Egyptian soldiers recover and begin to fight back. The Sherden bodyguard of the Pharaoh deploy to block any Hittite advance on the royal enclosure. The royal princes are moved to the eastern end of the camp for their protection.*

EG ⊠ XXXX
RAMESES II

Egyptian counter-attack

Plain of Qadesh

Shabtuna

Al-Mukadiyah

2 *Rameses dons his battle armour and rapidly leads out a number of squadrons of his chariotry via the eastern gate of the camp to counter-attack the Hittites.*
3 *With the Hittite attention seemingly fixed on the camp and the lure of the booty within, the Egyptian force is able to deploy and attack the dense mass of enemy chariotry with relative impunity. Rameses and his men pour a withering fire into the tightly packed ranks of the now very slow-moving Hittites. With their own momentum spent, and now under fierce attack, the*

Hittites panick and begin to disengage and retreat south.
4 *With the Egyptian chariots in pursuit, the Hitites retreat as fast as their rapidly tiring chariot teams allow, back towards the Al-Mukadiyah.*

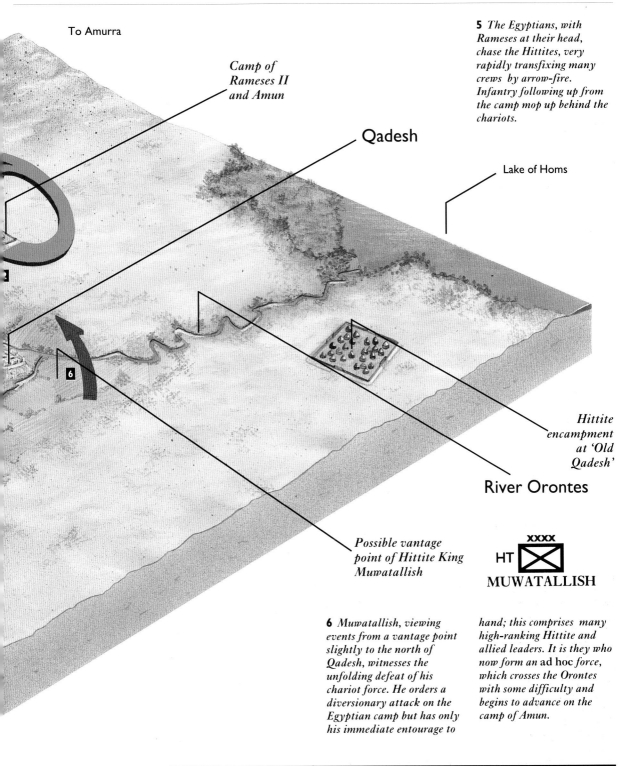

To Amurra

Camp of
Rameses II
and Amun

Qadesh

Lake of Homs

5 *The Egyptians, with Rameses at their head, chase the Hittites, very rapidly transfixing many crews by arrow-fire. Infantry following up from the camp mop up behind the chariots.*

Hittite
encampment
at 'Old
Qadesh'

River Orontes

Possible vantage
point of Hittite King
Muwatallish

HT ⊠ xxxx
MUWATALLISH

6 *Muwatallish, viewing events from a vantage point slightly to the north of Qadesh, witnesses the unfolding defeat of his chariot force. He orders a diversionary attack on the Egyptian camp but has only his immediate entourage to* hand; *this comprises many high-ranking Hittite and allied leaders. It is they who now form an ad hoc force, which crosses the Orontes with some difficulty and begins to advance on the camp of Amun.*

THE BATTLE OF QADESH

Phase Two: The Egyptian counter-attack and the Hittite second crossing of the River Orontes

but had in reality embarked upon a major reconnaissance of the camp of Amun to ascertain the exact size of the Egyptian force raises profound implications for other aspects of the accepted view of the battle. Of these the 'stand of Rameses', alone and abandoned by his chariotry, stands high in the ranks of tall stories. While the Bulletin proceeds to speak of the Hittite force as simply 'the host of the Hatti enemy', the Poem details that Rameses, 'found 2,500 chariots hemming him in on his outer side'. This figure, quoted with uncritical abandon by nearly all commentators of the battle, is quite fanciful. This much can be ascertained from a consideration of the length of time required by such a large force to cross the ford. A simple mathematical formula is sufficient to make the point. Allowing just one minute for each chariot to cross the ford (and it would certainly have taken longer than that!), it would have taken the 2,500 Hittite vehicles more than 41 hours to complete the task. Even if two chariots crossed together the point would still be well made, notwithstanding the halving of the time taken! The principle is also relevant to the second wave of 1,000 chariots where a mere $16\frac{1}{2}$ hours would have been required to effect the crossing.

Even if we accept these figures at face value, how was it that the Egyptian camp survived at all if such numbers of chariots were involved? The first wave of 2,500 Hittite chariots would have been more than adequate to have swamped the encampment whatever the degree of resistance Rameses and his available chariotry could have put up. We are dealing in the Poem with figures that are in reality the total for the

▲ *Of the nineteen allied and vassal states present with the Hittites and listed in the Qadesh inscriptions of Rameses II, the leaders of twelve of them are illustrated in this section of a relief from Luxor. None is specifically identified on the relief itself although the manner of dress, weaponry carried and hair style have allowed some to be tentatively identified with the later images of captured 'Sea Peoples' found on the walls of the temple of Rameses III at Medinet Habu.*

▶ *Again from the Rameseum, this photograph shows Pharaoh's chariot,*

albeit only the front legs of his team in the top left-hand corner, attacking a mass of Hittite chariotry. Many of the Hittites lie dead, pinioned by the long arrows fired from the Egyptian composite bows. The numbers of the dead were so great that in the Poem Rameses states, 'I caused the field to grow white (Gardiner uses 'light') for those of the land of Hatti.' making a reference to the long, light-coloured garment worn by many Hittite charioteers. Certainly not all wore the long scale armour shirts. The light-coloured garment may well have been fairly thick textile armour.

full chariot forces available to the Hittites for the Qadesh campaign and not in any way the number of chariots which Rameses actually fought. Positing a much smaller initial Hittite chariot force, it still would have been sufficient to have effected the disintegration of P'Re and also to have severely compromised the Egyptian position at the camp of Amun. The pictorial reliefs of the battle show only Hittite chariots and their three-man crews in combat with the Egyptians. Many of the Syrian allies of Hatti, however, deployed 'mariyannu', chariotry

◀ *In the process of executing the reliefs at the Rameseum a number of changes were introduced by the artist which necessitated translating images originally of Egyptian charioteers into Hittites. They are therefore examples of palimpsests, for the earlier work can clearly be seen. While the artist modified the shields to represent those of the type employed by Hittites, the number of crew remained* as for the Egyptian vehicle.

▲ *From the Rameseum, an excellent view of an Egyptian chariot racing into combat. Unusually in this case the 'seneny' or archer is holding forth the shield rather than the kedjen. Clearly shown is the grab rail extending forward from the top of the cab.*

derived from the Hurrian military tradition with two-man vehicles, using tactics more akin to those of the Egyptians, and these would in all probability have been deployed in their own units and not mixed with those of the Hittites. Those encountered by Pharaoh in the initial wave were in all probability therefore an exclusively Hittite force and this

requires that their numbers were as low as 500 chariots — a much more credible figure! The inability of the mass of the chariotry of Amun to react to this attack because of their unpreparedness for combat would nevertheless have meant that Pharaoh and the smaller Egyptian force that did manage to engage would have perceived themselves as, in some real sense, 'fighting the whole chariotry of the Hittite army'. This in no way demeans the 'stand of Rameses'. There can be no doubting that his prompt action in leading such chariot forces as were available for the counter-attack prevented the destruction of Amun. The excessive embellishment discernible in the accounts cannot deny the remarkable leadership displayed by Pharaoh for in a very real sense it was the personal bravery of Rameses that saved the day for the Egyptians.

The Hittite Second Wave

For Muwatallish, viewing the proceedings from a vantage-point near Qadesh, events were hardly turning out as had been expected. While it was clear that the bulk of the Egyptian army had yet to arrive, the precipitate action of his chariot force in attacking Pharaoh's camp had initiated combat before it was intended. Even so, Rameses had managed to retrieve the situation and was even now proceeding with some success to destroy a sizable number of the invaluable Hittite chariotry. Without assistance very few of the chariots dispatched a short time before would return. Matters urgently required that a diversion be created to take pressure off the retreating troops and draw Rameses back toward his camp.

With so few troops available, the Hittite king had only his entourage to hand. These had joined him to view the proceedings unfolding on the plain below, and were no doubt the last to expect to end up in combat. It was to these Muwatallish now turned with the request that they form a chariot force with a view to crossing the river and assaulting Rameses' camp. Among them were some of the foremost men of the Hittite army, including 'children and brothers' of the king and a number of the leaders of the allied contingents. Without hesitation, in loyalty to their Lord, the chariots were mustered into an *ad hoc* force and made off to cross the river at a point fairly close to Pharaoh's camp.

Passage of the Orontes was made with some difficulty, but having concentrated on the far side the force began to advance at a rapid pace towards the eastern end of the camp. Barely had the first Hittite chariots begun to penetrate the encampment than they were assaulted in a furious fashion by a body of Egyptian and allied chariotry that had appeared totally unexpectedly from the north. The long-awaited Ne'arin had finally arrived and at the moment of direst need for Pharaoh. Having divested themselves of their slower moving infantry which lay some miles to the rear along the line of march, the chariotry had stormed on to join Pharaoh. With his own surviving chariotry only now beginning to recover from seeing off the first Hittite force to the south of the camp, no appreciable forces were left to defend his own vulnerable encampment wherein were sheltering the royal princes and household! Later, Pharaoh would have inscribed on the walls of his mortuary temple at Thebes, '... the Ne'arin broke into the host of the wretched Fallen one of Hatti as they were entering the camp of Pharaoh

and the servants of His Majesty killed them...'

In a repetition of Rameses' rout of the first wave of chariotry, the Ne'arin unleashed massed volleys of arrows into the ranks of the Hittites who, unable to close with their enemy, could not defend themselves. The Hittite force visibly wavered, then began to retreat, its own passage back to the river made doubly horrendous by the appearance from the south of Pharaoh and elements of his chariotry (including possibly lead elements from Ptah). In a running battle all the way back to the river the Egyptians poured a withering fire from their composite bows into the now rapidly depleting Hittite ranks whose passage was marked by a wrack of smashed and crashed vehicles and a litter of white-shrouded bodies. Desperate to save their lives the leading charioteers plunged into the Orontes in a fatalistic bid to escape the rapidly closing Egyptians. A chaos of men, horses and chariots soon marked the recrossing of the Hittite force, with some among them lucky enough to regain the far bank while others were washed away by the current or dragged down by the weight of their armour.

With the retreat of the last of the Hittite chariotry to the east bank of the Orontes, the combat was to all intents over. Pharaoh retired to the wreckage of his camp, while all over the plain infantry hacked off the hands of the Hittite dead so as to allow the scribes to compile lists of the numbers of the Hittite fallen. To these were added the prisoners, many of whom had been recovered from the wrecked chariotry of the second Hittite assault. As with the dead, it was clear that there were many of high rank and status among them. The arrival of the corps of Ptah late in the day was matched by the slow trickling into the camp of many of the soldiers of Amun and

▶ *The Egyptian artists have gone to great trouble to depict the full infantry strength of the Hittites drawn up in front of Qadesh, top right of the picture. None of these troops was committed to battle and if the reasoning offered in the text is correct they were possibly not present at all, but rather still in camp to the north-west of the city. Shown clearly in the bottom left-hand corner are Hittite charioteers being hauled from the water, having been chased there by the Egyptian chariotry.*

1 *Having traversed the Orontes, the second Hittite column begins its approach to the Egyptian camp.*
2 *This coincides with the fortuitous arrival of the Ne'arin troops, who, having traversed Amurru via the Eleutheros valley, assault the second Hittite wave as it attacks the camp.*

3 *Recoiling in the face of this unexpected assault, the Hittite column disengages and begins a rapid flight back towards the Orontes in some disarray and panic.*

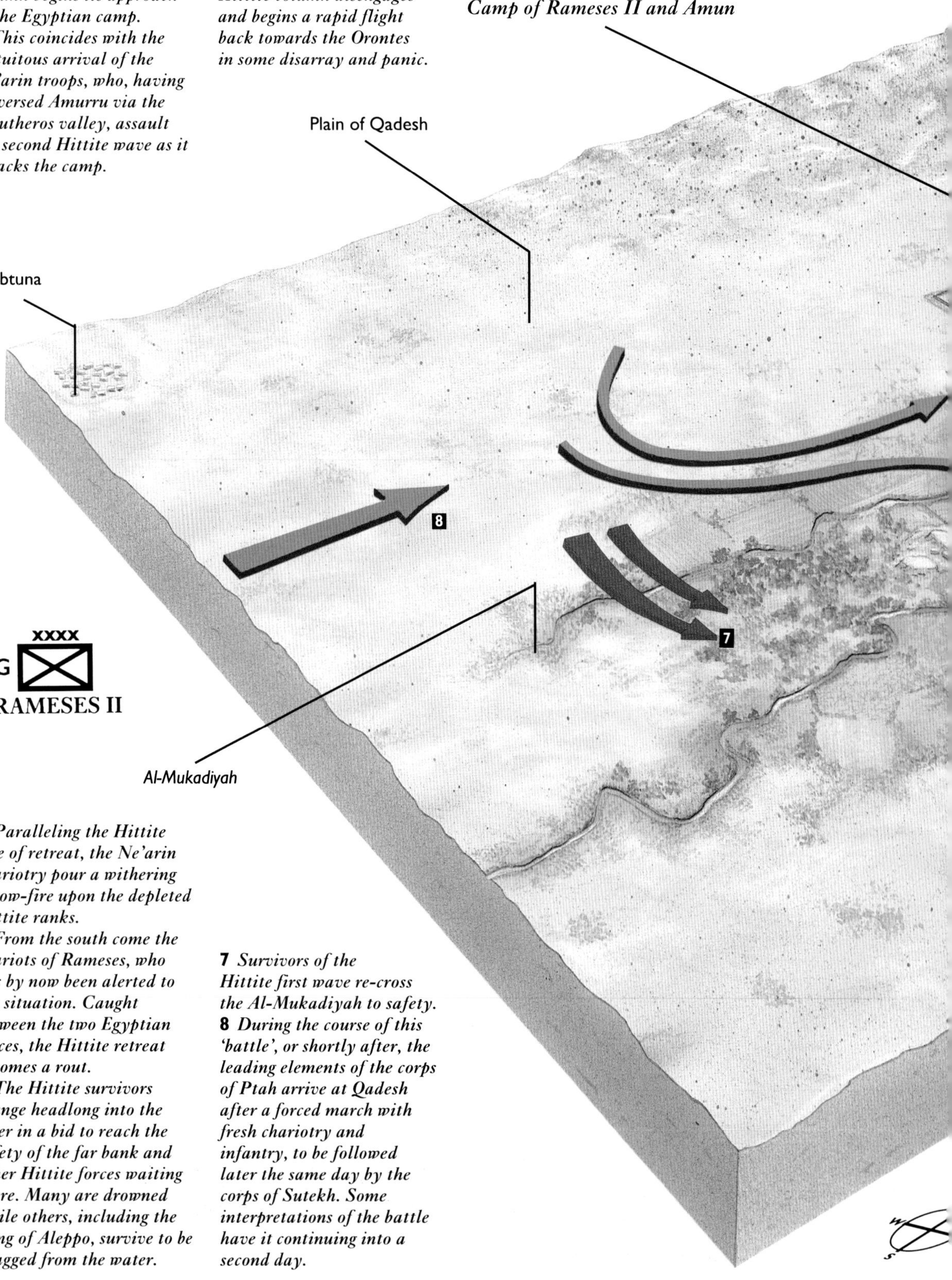

Camp of Rameses II and Amun

Plain of Qadesh

Shabtuna

EG
xxxx
⊠
RAMESES II

8

7

Al-Mukadiyah

4 *Paralleling the Hittite line of retreat, the Ne'arin chariotry pour a withering arrow-fire upon the depleted Hittite ranks.*
5 *From the south come the chariots of Rameses, who has by now been alerted to the situation. Caught between the two Egyptian forces, the Hittite retreat becomes a rout.*
6 *The Hittite survivors plunge headlong into the river in a bid to reach the safety of the far bank and other Hittite forces waiting there. Many are drowned while others, including the King of Aleppo, survive to be dragged from the water.*

7 *Survivors of the Hittite first wave re-cross the Al-Mukadiyah to safety.*
8 *During the course of this 'battle', or shortly after, the leading elements of the corps of Ptah arrive at Qadesh after a forced march with fresh chariotry and infantry, to be followed later the same day by the corps of Sutekh. Some interpretations of the battle have it continuing into a second day.*

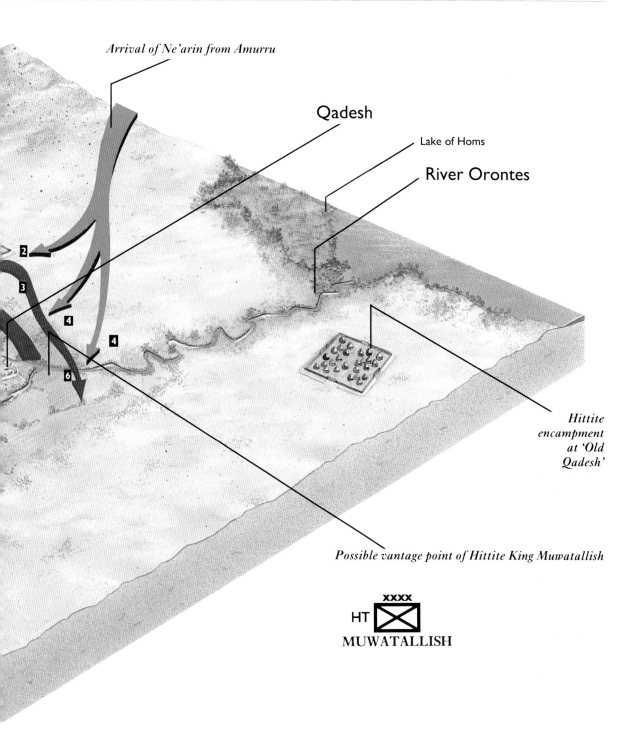

Arrival of Ne'arin from Amurru

Qadesh

Lake of Homs

River Orontes

2

3

4

4

6

Hittite encampment at 'Old Qadesh'

Possible vantage point of Hittite King Muwatallish

HT **XXXX** ⊠
MUWATALLISH

THE BATTLE OF QADESH

Phase Three: The Hittites' second attack and the intervention of Ne'arin

P'Re who had been 'discomfited' by the respective Hittite assaults. Their fate, however, as indeed that of the Egyptian campaign itself, now waited on the pronouncement of Pharaoh. Rameses had listened in silence to the congratulations of his senior officers on his personal prowess in the battle but had then subjected them to a withering tongue lashing and had given vent to his wrath on the pitiful conduct of his troops in the face of the enemy. As 'Use-mare Setpenre, Rameses Meryamun sat on his gold throne, brooding in his tent long into the night, there were many who sensed they had much to fear on the morrow.

Excursus Two

That the second wave of Hittite chariots was sent to attack Rameses' encampment in order to draw off pressure from those of their kind in the south of the plain cannot be seriously doubted. It was fortuitous for Rameses and decidedly unlucky for the Hittites that their penetration of the eastern end of the

▲Amid the battle scene is to be found a mounted rider no doubt carrying information or orders to some part of the battle-field. Immediately beneath him is a trans-fixed Hittite warrior clearly identifiable by the long hair that prompted Rameses to refer to them disparagingly as 'women soldiers'. In the Abu Simbel reliefs it is a mounted rider who is seen approaching the corps of Ptah. The text associated with the relief states, 'The scout of Pharaoh being come to hurry on the army of Ptah. There was said to them: "Go ahead, Pharaoh your Lord stands in the battle quite alone."'

encampment was being effected at exactly the same time as the Ne'arin were making their appearance on the scene. It would seem that their existence was totally unbeknown to the Hittites. Much speculation has been expended on the identity of this 'Egyptian' unit. The difficulty arises mainly from the imprecise meaning of the term Ne'arin. One of its principal uses comes from its association with the 'Semitic' background of those of whom it is

normally employed. The presumption has therefore been that they were a Canaanite *mariyannu* detachment in the service of Pharaoh. However the view has also been offered that they are identical with the '... first battle-force out of all the leaders of the army, and they were upon the shore of the Land of Amor' spoken of in the Poem.

Indeed, the depiction of the arrival of the Ne'arin at Qadesh in the Luxor reliefs shows them driving chariots of Egyptian style and employing the same tactics. A credible case has been offered for their being identified with the fourth army corps of 'Sutekh', the Semitic connotation being in the allusion to its title and possibly the larger numbers of Semitic troops serving in its ranks. Indeed, the sweep through Amurru via the Eleutheros valley may have been designed not only to steady Benteshina but to ensure the presence of his own chariotry at Qadesh. The vagueness of the position with which Sutekh is spoken of in the inscriptions lends credibility to the Ne'arin being identified with that corps.

▲In the wake of the Egyptian counter-attack on the second wave of Hittite chariotry, many of the crews ended up being driven back into the Orontes. This image from the Rameseum with its attached commentary shows, '... The wretched Chief of Khaleb (Aleppo) being emptied [of water] by his soldiers after His Majesty had thrown him into the water.'

It is clear that Muwatallish had little choice but to employ those immediate forces close to his person if he were to salvage any chariots from the first wave. That this was a scratch force seems very likely given the names of high-ranking figures in the Hittite army slain and captured and listed in the Rameseum. It seems reasonable to infer that under normal circumstances such a large number of dignitaries would not have fought in the battle had the mass of ordinary chariotry been available. This hypothesis is further strengthened if it is argued that, contrary to the inscriptions and reliefs, the mass of Hittite infantry was not present on this occasion either. The notion that Muwatallish had brought his infantry but not his chariotry is untenable. The absence of one implies the lack of the other. Any small number of infantry present, perhaps to guard his person, could not have been employed for the task which the *ad hoc* chariot force was dispatched to serve.

There is a very great deal to suggest that Qadesh was far from being the great battle assumed and presented in so many other accounts. Indeed, neither Rameses nor Muwatallish fought the 'battle' each expected or had planned for. A completely unplanned series of events transformed a limited Hittite reconnaissance into a running combat that nevertheless came very close to destroying the camp of Amun and killing Pharaoh. But its consequences were much as if the proper battle had actually been fought. Notwithstanding the Egyptian recovery, the bravery of Pharaoh and the tactically superior showing of the Egyptian chariotry, the dislocation of his army dashed Pharaoh's wider strategic aspirations. It is in that sense that Rameses was defeated at Qadesh. Muwatallish and Hatti had triumphed by default!

◀ *Libyan archer. As with the Nubians, the Egyptians incorporated Libyan auxiliaries into their army. While some would have worn aspects of Egyptian dress, the archer shown here wears little save the leather phallus cover and cloak made from bull-hide or giraffe skin, which provided a modicum of protection against arrow fire. Hair was plaited, with an ostrich feather for decoration. (Angus McBride)*

AFTERMATH

In many accounts of Qadesh the events of Day 11 are presumed to have involved a resumption of the battle. This derives from a particular interpretation of the text of the Poem and assumes that the enemies described therein are the Hittites. There is much however to suggest a different and more credible alternative. Far from identifying his enemies by the standard formula employed in the inscriptions of belonging to 'the Fallen one of Hatti', they are described simply as 'rebels'. Such a term is inappropriate to describe the Hittites and indeed nowhere

▼ *By cutting off one hand of a dead enemy and presenting it as a trophy to a scribe after the battle, an Egyptian soldier could demonstrate his prowess in combat and thus be awarded 'the gold of valour'. On the right of the photograph an Egyptian infantryman is about to take the right hand of a dying Hittite charioteer* *while on the left a Sherden has just begun to hack off the hand of a dead soldier. The taking of hands also allowed an assessment of the enemy dead.*

in any of the Rameside inscriptions are they described as such. In reality, these rebels were none other than the troops of Amun and P'Re who, having 'abandoned' Rameses on the field of battle, had broken the specific and reciprocal relationship that existed between Pharaoh and his soldiers. Having marshalled those whom he called 'rebels' in ranks as if for battle, he states that: '... My Majesty prevailed against them and I killed among them and did not relax, they sprawling before my horses and lying down in their blood in one place'. Those whom Rameses had killed were none other than his own men! What is without doubt the earliest document-

▲ Hittite dead litter the field in another picture taken from the Ramese-um. This illustrates in detail the Hittite 'field of the dead' seen on the last but one photograph, but extending above and to its right . Careful scrutiny of this picture will place the forelegs of Rameses' team in the bottom left-hand corner.

ed example of what the Romans referred to as 'decimation' was carried out on the Plain of Qadesh, in all probability in full and intended view of Muwatallish.

The Poem would have us believe that it was this

ruthless demonstration against his own troops that led the Hittite king to proffer a truce to Rameses. Notwithstanding the psychological impact the spectacle must have made, Muwatallish clearly had his own reasons for coming forward with the proposal. The losses among his own chariotry had been in the primary offensive arm of the Hittite force. As such, the impact on his chariot strength as well as on the morale of the remaining chariot units must have been profound. Even more so was the impact of the loss of many of the leading men of the expedition in the second wave. The premature initiation of battle on the previous day now precluded his exploiting to any advantage his early arrival at Qadesh. The advent of the other Egyptian corps of Ptah and Sutekh meant that Rameses now possessed a sizable force, but not enough to force the issue and win any battle that might now transpire. Gone to the winds were pharaonic aspirations to invade northern Syria — at least in the short term! Qadesh was safe in Hittite hands and as Rameses, given his losses, was in no position to remain in Syria, he would have no choice but to return to Egypt. Under such conditions Amurru would be bound to fall into the Hittite lap (indeed shortly thereafter Benteshina was taken captive to Hatti). Why then expend men and *matériel* if most of his strategic ambitions for this campaign could be realized, albeit by default? Indeed the Hittite monarch had every reason for thinking that should Rameses accept his proposal, Pharaoh would thus reveal his hand as one of weakness! Furthermore, the maintenance of a Hittite army in being was vital, for there can be no doubt-

▼ *Some sixteen years after Qadesh and the long cold war between the Nilotic empire and that of Hatti, a peace treaty was concluded between the two great powers. Inscribed on silver tablets the clauses, many pertaining to the demarcation of the boundary between the respective empires in Syria, was concluded with the declaration that they would not go to war with each other again. Of the borders in Syria, Egypt accepted that Qadesh and Amurru and the northern lands were lost forever. This is a graphic of a clay tablet bearing a copy of the treaty in Babylonian cuneiform, the lingua franca of diplomacy in the Ancient Near East, which was uncovered at the former Hittite capital Hattusas (Bogazkoy) in modern Turkey.*

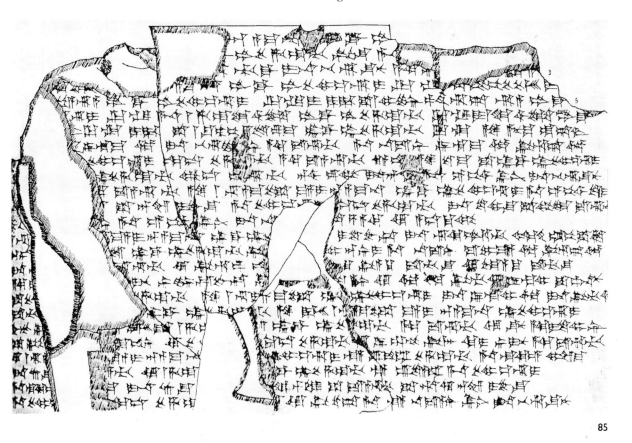

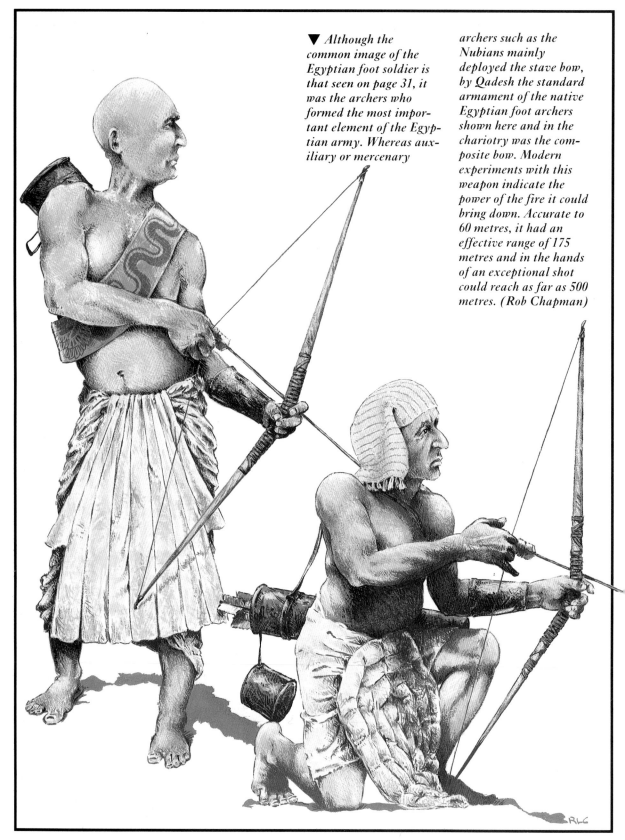

▼ *Although the common image of the Egyptian foot soldier is that seen on page 31, it was the archers who formed the most important element of the Egyptian army. Whereas auxiliary or mercenary archers such as the Nubians mainly deployed the stave bow, by Qadesh the standard armament of the native Egyptian foot archers shown here and in the chariotry was the composite bow. Modern experiments with this weapon indicate the power of the fire it could bring down. Accurate to 60 metres, it had an effective range of 175 metres and in the hands of an exceptional shot could reach as far as 500 metres. (Rob Chapman)*

Aftermath

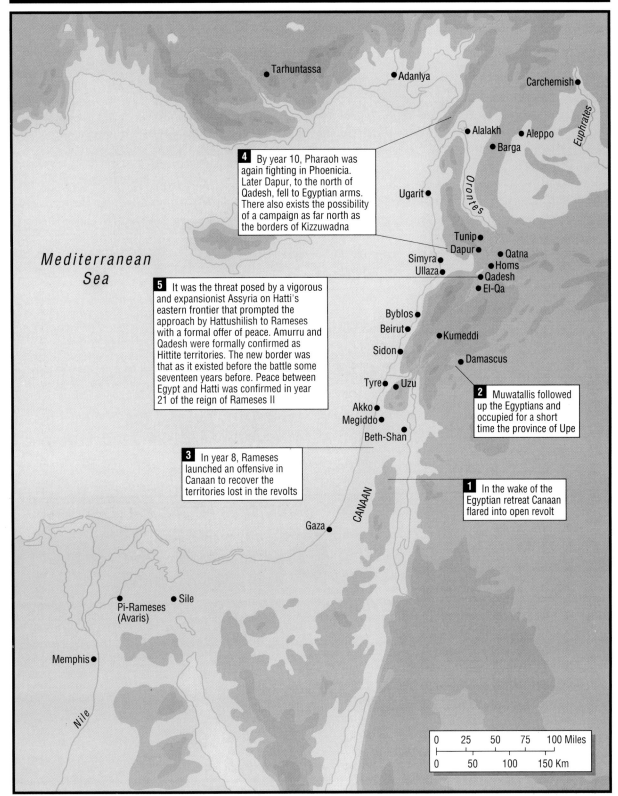

Tarhuntassa

Adanlya

Carchemish

Alalakh
Aleppo
Barga

4 By year 10, Pharaoh was again fighting in Phoenicia. Later Dapur, to the north of Qadesh, fell to Egyptian arms. There also exists the possibility of a campaign as far north as the borders of Kizzuwadna

Ugarit

Orontes

Euphrates

Mediterranean Sea

Tunip
Dapur
Simyra
Ullaza
Qatna
Homs
Qadesh
El-Qa

5 It was the threat posed by a vigorous and expansionist Assyria on Hatti's eastern frontier that prompted the approach by Hattushilish to Rameses with a formal offer of peace. Amurru and Qadesh were formally confirmed as Hittite territories. The new border was that as it existed before the battle some seventeen years before. Peace between Egypt and Hatti was confirmed in year 21 of the reign of Rameses II

Byblos
Beirut
Kumeddi
Sidon
Damascus

Tyre
Uzu

Akko
Megiddo
Beth-Shan

2 Muwatallis followed up the Egyptians and occupied for a short time the province of Upe

3 In year 8, Rameses launched an offensive in Canaan to recover the territories lost in the revolts

1 In the wake of the Egyptian retreat Canaan flared into open revolt

CANAAN

Gaza

Pi-Rameses (Avaris)
Sile

Memphis

Nile

0	25	50	75	100 Miles
0		50	100	150 Km

ing that Muwatallish was acutely conscious that the vassal kingdoms of Anatolia and Syria in addition to Adad-Nirari of Assyria were keenly awaiting reports on the outcome of the battle. Hatti had nothing to gain by fighting on and much to gain by a cessation of hostilities.

In the wake of the truce that followed Rameses and his army repaired to Egypt, accompanied so it is said by whistles and catcalls as they passed through the towns of Canaan. As if to compound the obvious Hittite advantage, Muwatallish trailed the withdrawing Egyptian army and occupied, albeit temporarily, the province of Upe. The news of Qadesh, of the perceived failure of the Egyptian army and the humiliation of the overbearing Pharaoh as sufficient to raise the whole of Canaan in revolt even as the army entered Egypt. Notwith-

standing the Egyptian recovery on the battlefield, the fallout from Qadesh would result in Rameses spending many years reimposing Egyptian rule in Canaan and Syria.

When ultimately Egypt and Hatti came to terms in the twenty-first year of Rameses' reign, the territorial settlement saw the Nilotic kingdom reconciled to the permanent loss of Amurru, Qadesh and the aspirations to northern Syria. Under the aegis of Re and the Storm God of Hatti, the treaty was '... to make it a prosperous peace, and he shall make excellent the brotherhood between the great king, the king of Egypt, and the great king of Hatti, his brother, for ever and ever!' Until the demise of the Hittite empire in 1190, the treaty remained unbroken and the Ancient Near East witnessed eighty years of remarkable peace and prosperity.

◀ *It was in the thirty-fourth year of Rameses' reign that he married the daughter of Hattushilish III, King of Hatti. An outward sign of the stability of Egyptian-Hittite accord, Pharaoh was in his fifties when the marriage union was concluded. While it is doubtful that the Hittite king ever visited Egypt, he is necessarily shown with his hands upraised in supplication with those of his daughter as he approaches Pharaoh. Even to the end royal propagandists would never suggest that Pharaoh was anything other than the superior ruler. Rameses was evidently very pleased with his Hittite bride: 'Her [Egyptian] name was proclaimed as, "Queen Maat-Hor-Nefrure", may she live daughter of the Great Ruler of Hatti, and daughter of the Great Queen of Hatti.' Egypt and Hatti remained at peace until the Sea Peoples swept away the great northern power in c.1190.*

CHRONOLOGY

Notwithstanding the continuing debate concerning the reliability of dating this period, the substance of which falls outside the domain of this title, that employed within is the same as used by the *Cambridge Ancient History*. This also allows continuity with the chronology in the Osprey Elite title of *New Kingdom Egypt* by the same author. Readers should be aware that whereas this places Qadesh in 1300, other texts, using a 'lower' date, place it in approximately 1275.

*c.*1674: The Hyksos invaders take control of Lower Egypt. Reduce rest of kingdom to vassaldom.

*c.*1570: Amosis crowned king. Establishes the 18th 'Theban' Dynasty. Continues war of 'liberation' against the Hyksos.

*c.*1565: Hyksos invaders finally cleared from Egypt. The Nilotic kingdom becomes tacit overlord of Canaan and the Levant as far north as the River Euphrates.

*c.*1546-1526: Possible military campaign by Amenophis I in Syria.

*c.*1525-*c.*12: Tuthmosis I leads the army into Syria and engages the forces of a nascent Kingdom of Mitanni. Sets up a stela on the banks of the Euphrates. This marks the northernmost point of Egyptian expansion in New Kingdom.

*c.*1482-50: Tuthmosis III undertakes seventeen campaigns in Canaan and Syria to impose Egyptian rule. In his campaign of Year 33 Tuthmosis invades Mitanni proper inflicting on that power a major defeat that raises the prestige and reputation of the Egyptian army to the foremost of that in the Ancient Near East. Even before his death the power of the Nilotic kingdom in Syria is on the wain in the face of a resurgent Mitanni.

*c.*1450-*c.*25: Amenophis II campaigns in northern Syria in order to reassert Egyptian rule, but Mitanni manages to retain dominance in the region. A resurgent Hatti prompts approaches by Mitanni to establish lasting 'brotherhood' with Egypt.

*c.*1425-17: Treaty between Egypt and Mitanni concluded in reign of Tuthmosis IV. A clear demarcation of their respective empires in central Syria is the primary consequence. Egypt relinquishes claims to its former northern territories. These borders are viewed by Egypt as marking the true boundaries of her empire in Asia. Two generations of peace follow.

*c.*1380-50: Under their king Suppiluliumas, in two major wars the Hittites effectively destroy the Kingdom of Mitanni and their northern Syrian empire. Egypt loses Ugarit, Qadesh and Amurru. Egypt now shares its northern borders with the Hittite empire.

*c.*1320-18: The accession of Rameses I marks the beginning of the 19th Dynasty and a commitment to the recovery of Egypt's 'lost' territories in Syria.

*c.*1318-04: Seti I begins the process of recovering Qadesh and Amurru. Although the latter territory seems to have stayed firmly in the Hittite camp, Qadesh is recovered by the new pharaoh for Egypt for the last time. Nevertheless, it is recovered through treaty by Hatti even before Seti's death.

1304-01: Rameses II ascends the throne, but not until 1301 does Benteshina, King of Amurru, repudiate his vassal treaty with Hatti and defect to Egypt. A rapid campaign by Rameses in that year draws Amurru firmly into the Egyptian camp. Muwatallish, King of Hatti, prepares for war.

THE BATTLE OF QADESH

Day 9, second month of summer season, Year 5 (late April 1300): The Egyptian army leaves Egypt to begin its march to Qadesh on the Orontes.

Day 9, third month of summer season, Year 5 (late May 1300): Rameses and the advance corps of Amun encamp to the south of Qadesh. Unbeknown to them the Hittite army is already encamped in the vicinity. The Egyptians only become aware of their presence in the evening when Hittite scouts are captured and interrogated. Pharaoh dispatches Vizier to hurry on the army.

Day 10: The corps of P'Re is attacked by a large Hittite reconnaissance detachment and blown to the winds as it marches across the Plain of Qadesh heading for the camp of Rameses and Amun. The Hittite chariot force attacks the Egyptian camp, lured by the great booty within. Rameses manages to save the day with a small chariot detachment. Having forced the Hittites to retire with great losses, a relief Hittite force is dispatched by Muwatallish across the Orontes to alleviate pressure on the first force. As the second detachment attacks Pharaoh's camp they are themselves surprised by the Ne'arin, a detached force of Egyptian and allied chariotry. The Hittites retreat leaving many dead. Others drown attempting to escape across the river. The arrival of the corps of Ptah late in the day bol-sters the strength of the Egyptian army at Qadesh. Combat ceases.

Day 11: Pharaoh, making an example of those whom he believes to have shown cowardice on the previous day, executes a large number of men from the corps of Amun and P'Re in full view of the Hittites. A truce offered by Muwatallish is accepted by Rameses. The Egyptian Army retreats to Egypt and the Hittites occupy the province of Upe. Virtually the whole empire in Canaan and Syria rises in rebellion as Qadesh is perceived as a major Hittite victory. Rameses spends many years reasserting Egyptian rule in these territories.

*c.*1283: Egypt and Hatti finally come to terms and settle their borders in Syria. Hatti retains Qadesh and Amurru and both remain within the Hittite empire until its demise in *c.*1190 at the hands of 'The Sea Peoples'.

▶ *Subsequent to the Battle of Qadesh the two accounts which record the event in some length together with their supporting pictorial reliefs were recorded in multiple copies on temples throughout Egypt. The two accounts known as the 'Bulletin' and the 'Poem' were inscribed seven and eight times respectively at the Rameseum, Abydos, Karnak, Abu Simbel and here at Luxor. They are the main source for the battle.*

A GUIDE TO FURTHER READING

ALDRED, Cyril. *The Egyptians*. Thames & Hudson, 1984

BAINES AMD MALEK. *Atlas of Ancient Egypt*. Equinox Books, 1983

Cambridge Ancient History. Part 11, 2A, 1975

GARDINER, Sir Alan. *The Kadesh Inscriptions of Rameses II*. Ashmolean Museum, 1960

GOEDICKE, Hans (ed). *Perspectives on the Battle of Kadesh*. Halgo Inc, 1985

GURNEY, O.R. *The Hittites*. Penguin Books, 1952

Kitchen, K. *Pharaoh Triumphant*. Aris & Phillips Ltd, 1982

MACQUEEN, J. G. *The Hittites*. Thames & Hudson, 1975

MURNANE, W.J. *The Road to Qadesh*. University of Chicago, 1985

NEWBY, P.H. *The Warrior Pharaohs*. Faber, 1980

REDFORD, D.B. *Egypt, Canaan and Israel in Ancient Times*. Princeton University Press, 1992

WARGAMING QADESH

If one chooses to wargame the whole campaign of Year 5, then certainly an interesting map game should result. Also several 'Committee games' could be staged with the players representing Pharaoh and his divisional commanders, or Muwatallish and his allies and vassals. Arguments on the Egyptian side should revolve around whether to direct the main effort up the Beka'a valley (as in the historical prototype) or along the coast (as in the campaign of the previous year) or split the effort between the two. On the Hittite side it might be a question of whether to approach the wargame more aggressively, and perhaps advance the army south of Qadesh.

Of course if the players are allowed free rein in this, then the chances of their campaign culminating in a battle bearing much resemblance to the historical Qadesh are slim. For those interested in logistics, however, this may not be too great a sacrifice, and such questions as 'What is the maximum load and speed of a baggage donkey?' may for some have a fascination of their own. (About 100lb and 2mph incidentally!)

If it is desired to refight the whole campaign rather than just the battle of Qadesh, then study of recent Arab-Israeli Wars and, more particularly, Allenby's Palestine campaign of 1917–18 would pay dividends. If one wanted to disguise the scenario, then a 1917 setting with Turkish and British or ANZAC cavalry replacing the chariots would fit the bill.

The Eve of Battle

Much of what was said above can be applied to the situations of the two armies the night before the battle. Committee games could be staged which could result in the manner of the Egyptian advance being changed: perhaps Pharaoh would be persuaded to be more cautious. Similarly the Hittites

might opt for a more conventional battle line. Perhaps Qadesh itself might be stormed. But all these options would lose the flavour of the historical battle, and that would be a pity because it is virtually unique in ancient military history. Let us therefore assume that the wargamers wish to refight only the battle of Qadesh itself – or that the campaign umpire has so contrived the committee games as to drive them willy-nilly to the vicinity of Qadesh in the dispositions – both physical and mental – of their historical counterparts!

The Battle Itself

Because of the arrival on the battlefield of so many forces not present at the start of the action, at different times and from different directions, and the consequent 'see-sawing' of the fortunes of battle, Qadesh presents a most interesting recreation for the wargamer. It is far more interesting than the stereotyped line-ups of Greek and Roman battlefields, and in fact has more the flavour of many Napoleonic battles, with the Emperor's Grand Tactical design of the concentration of separately marching corps on the battlefield itself. We should always bear in mind that Napoleon planned things this way, while for Rameses it was rather more in the nature of fortuitous accident. But the end result is the same: a ding-dong, to-and-fro battle, which should allow an exciting boardgame or tabletop game with miniatures.

Bearing the above in mind, it is most important to set up the wargame in such a way that the essential flavour of the historical battle is retained. In his book *Ancient Battles for Wargamers* (Argus Books, 1977) the late Charles Grant described a refight of Qadesh in which the division of P'Re turned to face the Hittite ambushing force and, after a hard slog, beat them off virtually unaided! Most sets of wargame rules will (rightly) classify the Egyptians as regular, well-trained troops of average or above average morale and – unless some special 'Qadesh factors' are grafted on to commercial rules – the above misfortune could befall any tabletop refight.

How can we be sure that our wargame will retain the essential features – and thus the excitement – of the battle, and not degenerate into just another nondescript 'Egyptians versus Hittites' game? The answer is to begin in the middle. Do not start the game with the Hittite chariot force bursting from cover to attack the flank of P'Re division. Start the game with P'Re and Amun already in rout – indeed most of them already routed out of the area represented by the tabletop; with the Hittite chariots scattered in pursuit, many of them approaching Pharaoh's camp; and with Rameses and his small force of Royal chariots and Sherden infantry ready to resist the onslaught. To be sure that they are not too easily overwhelmed (as in reality they were not) though seemingly so heavily outnumbered (as in reality they were) we must pay particular attention to the moral and physical state of the different bodies of troops involved in the battle at this point, and of those who are to enter the tabletop battlefield in the ensuing turns, and make sure that the rules we are using reflect them accurately.

But first let us consider the tabletop battlefield itself. Who is on it at the start of the battle, and who is going to enter it subsequently?

The Battlefield

First it should be a fairly long tabletop, not less than 12ft by 6ft for 25mm scale miniatures. The southern end of the table would represent a line above the northern edge of the forest of Robawi. The Egyptian division of Ptah should ultimately enter the battlefield here. Pharaoh's camp should be near, but not on, the northern edge of the table. The Sherden should be in the camp and Pharaoh's Royal chariotry just outside it, to the north. The Ne'arin troops should subsequently arrive in the north-west corner of the battlefield and any rallied units of the Amun and P'Re divisions should return via the northern edge.

The eastern side of the table would roughly denote the course of the River Orontes. The second force of Hittite chariots, 1,000 strong, should enter the battlefield here, just north of Qadesh, which can be represented on this edge of the table – or may be assumed to be just off-table if no suitable model is available. If Qadesh itself is represented, then obviously part of the Orontes will also have to be represented in this corner of the table, in which case Muwatallish and the main body of Hittite and allied infantry can also be put on-table for visual effect.

Apart from Pharaoh and his Household troops, the only Egyptians on the table at the start of the game should be some scattered remnants of P'Re division. Not all of this division would have fled northward through Pharaoh's camp. Strung out on the march, the tail of the column would more likely flee south towards the protection of the Ptah division; the centre of the column probably westward directly away from the immediate threat of the Hittite chariotry. Those chariots would also have spread out in pursuit of the scattered Egyptians, with probably most (but certainly not all) of them swinging north towards the Royal camp.

Let us now look at each force in turn and consider whether any special rules need to be devised to cater for its part in the battle.

The Forces

First, the Hittite ambush force of 2,500 chariots. (By the end of the battle the Egyptians had captured plenty of Hittite and allied leaders of high rank to interrogate, so we can be fairly sure that this figure is reasonably accurate. When exaggerating the Egyptian records of Qadesh usually refer to 'millions' or 'hundreds of thousands', '2500' is sufficiently conservative to have the ring of truth!) It was for long thought that the Hittite chariots had a crew of three men. This belief was based solely on a misinterpretation of the Egyptian records of Qadesh. The key passage (*Kadesh Inscriptions of Rameses II*, Sir Alan Gardiner, Oxford, 1960 p. 85) is: 'and he [Pharaoh] found 2,500 chariots hemming him in on his outer side, consisting of all the champions of the fallen ones of Khatti ... they being three men on a chariot acting as a unit ...'.

Reading Gardiner's notes on this passage, we find that 'consisting of' could equally well be 'with'; 'champions' is literally 'runners' [i.e., light infantry]; and 'acting as a unit' is literally 'they made unitings'. Now to us as military historians this phrase makes perfect sense: the Hittite chariotry 'made unitings' with their supporting light infantry, 'they being three men on a chariot' (but only two of them charioteers). (A depiction of a Hittite chariot by the Hittites themselves, discovered in Anatolia since Breasted's original translation of the Egyptian reliefs, shows only two crewmen.) To allow the infantry supports to keep pace with the chariots in their rapid advance against the flank of P'Re division, and subsequently on to Rameses' camp, they had to 'hitch a ride' (infantry were still doing it in the Second World War, on the backs of advancing tanks!).

This presents us with a problem, for virtually all commercial sets of wargame rules have no mechanism to adequately represent this tactic. Grafting on such a rule is usually very difficult because commercial rules usually have different ratios for the different arms. For example, in the popular Wargame Research Group rules 1 model infantry figure represents 20 real infantry, but 1 model chariot represents only 5 real ones; so one model infantry figure would have to support four model chariots – a difficult prospect! Probably the best solution is to go back to wargaming's 'cottage industry' roots and devise your own set of rules from scratch!

Historically it is quite possible (perhaps probable) that the morale of P'Re division cracked *before* the Hittite chariot force made contact with it. (Gardiner concedes that his translation [the Hittite chariotry] 'broke into' [P'Re] could equally be rendered 'overwhelmed'.) This would explain why fugitives, most of whom would have been on foot, were able to flee through Pharaoh's camp before the Hittite chariotry reached it – to do that they would have needed a head start!

For the purposes of our game it also means that a very large proportion of P'Re division, as well as the whole of Amun division, should be available for rallying should Pharaoh with his bodyguards and the freshly arrived Ne'arin troops do enough to stem the tide of the Hittite advance. Each move,

a morale test should be carried out for Egyptian units assumed to be routed off the northern edge of the board at the start of the game. The chances of their rallying and returning to battle should increase with each move that Pharaoh and the Ne'arin hold back the Hittite chariotry. However, should the Hittites be able to exit chariot units off the northern end of the board (simulating continuing pursuit) then the chances of the Egyptian troops rallying would be diminished.

Many commentators have expressed incredulity at Rameses' overthrow of the Hittite chariotry with so small a force. If we were considering a force of 2,500 fresh Hittite chariots, then such expressions would doubtless be correct. But that is a description of the Hittite chariots as they burst forth from behind Qadesh, where they had been hidden in ambush after crossing from the east side of the Orontes. After a fast canter (if not a hard gallop) – and some scattering – in pursuit of P'Re, it would be a diminished Hittite chariot force, coming up piecemeal with blown horses, which confronted the Pharaoh. We need not doubt Rameses' claim that he charged six times into battle. His bodyguard were élite troops; their horses were rested; coming up in a succession of straggling groups, the enemy chariots would almost certainly give way before them. As long as the Egyptians kept their formation and their discipline and did not succumb to pushing their pursuit too far, they would be able to rally and charge again. Nor must we forget the lure of the camp and its booty to distract many of the Hittites.

So, for the purposes of our game, the rules should give the Egyptian Royal bodyguard the following advantages: a morale bonus for being élite troops commanded by their sovereign in person; a bonus in mêlée for the same reasons; and a movement bonus for having fresh horses – probably the best horses in the Egyptian army. The Hittite chariotry should have a movement penalty for having tired horses; and a consequent morale penalty should they be charged while in such a state. The rules should allow chariot units to stand and 'breathe' their horses, which after a certain number of turns would then be fit enough to move and charge again without penalty.

Also at this stage of the game any Hittite chariot

unit coming near the Egyptian camp, but not within charge reach of Egyptian chariots, should have to take a morale test to see if they lose their discipline and start to loot the camp. Most rules have an 'uncontrolled advance' or similar category in their morale tables. Such a result in this instance would mean that that unit started looting. Looters should suffer very severe penalties in both morale and mêlée if attacked by either the Sherden troops in the camp or the Ne'arin troops when they arrive on the tabletop.

This brings us to the question of the Ne'arin. Just who they were has been a fraught question for Egyptologists. It is important for us to know for the purposes of the game, so that we can represent them with the correct troop types. The force has been variously identified as Asiatic auxiliaries or as the division of Sutekh, but with no evidence to support either contention. The line in the poem, 'and His Majesty had made the first battle-force out of all the leaders of his army, and they were upon the shore of the land of Amor', provides the best evidence. It would have been possible for Rameses to have split his force and send a detachment north via the coastal route into the land of Amor upon leaving Egypt. But such a force could not have been composed 'out of all the leaders of his army', because we know that he had his Household troops with him in his camp by Qadesh. Nor does the description fit the division of Sutekh, let alone Asiatic allies. The only logical time – indeed the only possible time – for Rameses to have left a composite force of his élite troops on the coast of Amor was at the end of the previous year's campaign, when the main army retired to winter quarters in Egypt. At the start of the next campaign these troops would be ordered to rendezvous with the main army at Qadesh.

For the purposes of our wargame, then, we must make the Ne'arin an élite and veteran force, with advantages in discipline and morale. This may also help explain the panic in the divisions of P'Re and Amun. If they had been stripped of many of their best soldiers at the end of the previous campaign, they would probably contain a higher than usual proportion of raw recruits, raised during the winter to fill the ranks. Anyone opting to begin refighting the battle of Qadesh from its historical start point

(the surprise attack by the Hittite chariots) should particularly note this possibility and give P'Re and Amun some morale disadvantages to reflect it.

Let us now look briefly at the second Hittite chariot force. The records tell us that it was 1,000 strong, and that its various contingents were led by many high-ranking Hittites (often of Royal blood) and allied chieftains. (Significantly they make no mention of three men per chariot when describing this force.) For the purposes of the wargame we should consider this force to be élite and therefore of high morale; not as well coordinated as the Egyptian forces, because of its polyglot composition; and unsupported by light infantry.

The final force we need to consider is the division of Ptah, which came up from the south. This would be a composite force of chariotry and infantry, like the other divisions. It too may have had some of its best troops seconded at the end of the previous campaign and replaced by recruits. Much has been made by commentators of the seemingly long time it took Ptah to reach Rameses, and discussion of this has always centred around how far south the unit must have been for it to have taken this time to come up. But all these computations have been geared to route marching rates of troops *not* in the presence of enemy forces. It is almost certain that the plain south of Qadesh and Rameses' camp would be swarming with Hittite chariotry. Ptah would therefore have had to move north in battle formation, continually skirmishing with groups of Hittites. Advancing in such conditions would undoubtedly be a slow process. If your wargames table is long enough, then the Ptah division could be deployed on-table from the start, fighting its own battle towards the Royal camp.

The Players

The game would be best played with at least three Egyptian commanders: Pharaoh, commanding his Household troops and any Amun or P'Re troops returning to the northern edge of the board; the commander of the Ne'arin troops, arriving at the north-west corner of the board fairly early in the battle; and the Vizier leading on the division of Ptah (and also taking under command any scattered remnants of P'Re that remain to the south).

The Hittites would also be handled best by at least three commanders: two with the first force of chariots and light infantry, one to handle events in the north against the Egyptian camp, the other in the south opposing the advance of Ptah; the third player would control the second force of chariots.

The game would be balanced if the arrival times of the initially off-table force were fixed by a non-playing umpire but not communicated to the players, so that an element of surprise remained. Otherwise, certainly if a non-playing umpire were not possible, the arrival times for these forces would have to be set out in a timetable, but with possible delays subject to some chance factor so that things would not be too predictable for the players.

Widening the Scope

Two forces not considered here are the main body of Hittite infantry (37,000 strong according to the Egyptian records) and the division of Sutekh. Neither made it to the historical battlefields; nor is there much chance of either making it on to a tabletop refight that adheres reasonably closely to the prototype. Most commentators accept that Sutekh was too far south to reach the battle in time. A few without a shred of evidence in support, equate it with the Ne'arin.

If we want to enter the realm of conjecture here is a suggestion that has some I.M.P. (Inherent Military *Possibility* in this case – to say *Probability* would be rather rash). Suppose that the Sutekh division carried on along the east bank of the Orontes, moving for a while due east before swinging back north. Two points could lend some support to such a theory. First the city of Qadesh was the main aim of the campaign. It had formerly been an Egyptian vassal but had gone over to the Hittite alliance. It was a politically influential state, and its geographical position made it a very important communications centre. The Egyptians wanted it back, and to isolate it they would ultimately have needed a force to block the eastern approaches on the other side of the Orontes. Second, the approach of such a force on the east bank of the river would provide a better reason for the seeming immobility of the main Hittite infantry

than any yet put forward. Wargaming is all about 'What if?', so we could certainly refight a Qadesh incorporating such dispositions on a somewhat larger tabletop or board. The game would then need at least one more player on each side – and would give the umpire a few more headaches in sorting out his timetable.

Whether the desultory fighting of the following day is worth wargaming would obviously depend on how closely the wargame had followed the historical prototype. Perhaps another 'Committee game' could be staged to allow the players themselves to decide if it would be worthwhile to resume the tabletop action.

Hardware

Qadesh has been produced as a boardgame. It appeared in issue 7 of the *American Command Magazine* (Nov–Dec 1990). A sheet of 168 die-cut cardboard counters and a 34in × 22in mapboard are provided as inserts; the rules are an integral part of the magazine, which also carries an article providing background information. Some of the background information may be erroneous, the map may be rather bland, and a few of the counters may represent units that are conjectural rather than historical; but you *are* wargamers! A couple of test plays, a few changes here and there and you will get a reasonable game out of it! The main criticism of the rules as they stand is that they make for a very slow game.

Miniatures are available in 25mm scale from a few manufacturers, notably Hinchcliffe Models, now available from Ellerburn Armies, Boxtree, Thornton Dale, near Pickering, North Yorks YO18 7SD; Garrison Figures, now available from S.K.T., 9 Wargrave Road, Twyford, Reading, Berks. RG10 9NY; and Essex Miniatures, Unit 1, Shannon Centre, Shannon Square, Thames Estuary Estate, Canvey Island, Essex SS8 0PE. The choice of Egyptians is fairly good; the Hittites are very sparsely covered. In 15mm, Donnington Miniatures, 15 Cromwell Road, Shaw, Newbury, Berks. RG13 2HE and Chariot Miniatures, 25 Broad Mead, Luton, Beds. LU3 1RX have ranges.